Under *Albany*

RON SILLIMAN has written and edited 25 books to date, most recently *Woundwood*. Between 1979 and 2004, Silliman wrote a single poem entitled *The Alphabet*. In addition to *Woundwood*, a part of *VOG*, volumes published thus far from that project have included *ABC*, *Demo to Ink*, *Jones*, *Lit*, *Manifest*, *N/O*, *Paradise*, *®*, *Toner*, *What* and *Xing*. He is the editor of the anthology, *In the American Tree* and the author of the critical book, *The New Sentence*. Silliman was a 2003 Literary fellow of the National Endowment for the Arts and was a 2002 Fellow of the Pennsylvania Arts Council as well as a Pew Fellow in the Arts in 1998. He lives in Chester County, Pennsylvania, with his wife and two sons, and works as a market analyst in the computer industry. His weblog on poetics, *Silliman's Blog*, has had over 170,000 visitors in its first two years.

Under *Albany*

Ron Silliman

SALT

CAMBRIDGE

PUBLISHED BY SALT PUBLISHING
PO Box 937, Great Wilbraham, Cambridge PDO CB1 5JX United Kingdom
PO Box 202, Applecross, Western Australia 6153

© Ron Silliman, 2004

The right of Ron Silliman to be identified as the
author of this work has been asserted by her in accordance
with Section 77 of the Copyright, Designs and Patents Act 1988.

First published 2004

Printed and bound in the United Kingdom by Lightning Source

Typeset in Swift 9.5 / 13

ISBN 1 84471 051 3 paperback

Covered based upon a photograph by Jeff Hurwitz.
Used with permission.

SP

1 3 5 7 9 8 6 4 2

For Colin and Jesse,
Later

Under *Albany*

Under *Albany*

If the function of writing is to "express the world."

Jon Arnold looks out over the straw-haired sea of fifth-graders directly into the dark eyes of Susan Hughes. Behind him, cordoned by both the furniture and the authority of the instructor's desk, Vance Teague, then in his sixth year of teaching at Marin Elementary, observes the latest in his unending string of small pedagogical experiments. Unlike dividing the classroom into teams and having them compete for grades, this one shows promise. Each Wednesday, students will be given one sheet of lined paper and a ballpoint pen—industrial strength, the point never retracting, virtually impossible to open, snap or chew through. The students are allotted one hour to write whatever they wish, whatever they might. There are no rules, and that *is* the rule.

On the following Wednesday, just before "writing hour," Teague, who had first met Arnold and myself while student-teaching kindergarten under the creaking but benevolent mentorship of Mrs. Seager, will select a handful of students whose writing in some fashion has "excelled," having them read them aloud to the class. This will be my first experience of The Reading.

Arnold, a sharp kid who frightened me because he was constantly pushing me and our mutual friend Timmy Johnson toward further and further transgressions of adult authority, stares into the intense smile of the partly Native American girl whose dark hair and faintly olive skin makes the pale northern European tones of the classroom visible to all. He begins to read. The subject of Arnold's paper—*how would a ten-year-old think of this?*—is the reaction of students hearing him (already typecast as one of the "wild kids") read aloud. Arnold's paper, which may have been shorter than this comment upon it forty years later, is a Swiftian satire on class relations . . . in all senses of that phrase. The students get the joke instantly. There is a lot of wincing and laughter and, at the end (and for the only time all school year), applause. I remember the humor as terrific, although cruel.[1]

I am transfixed. So much so, in fact, that I am unable to write a coherent sentence in the following hour that day and turn in a blank sheet of paper. A week later, I use the "free writing" period to attempt a piece that tries to switch literary genres sentence by sentence, essay one moment, science fiction the next. My effort disintegrates into garble. (Although in retrospect I realize that I somehow already knew what a genre was and that there were differences between them.) Teague is concerned. Within a matter of weeks, I am writing "novels," though, sitting on my narrow bed in the small room I shared with my younger brother, Cliff, longhand tales scrawled into thick notebooks ("the assassination of Hitler," "manned rocket flies behind moon only to disappear"). Within in a year, I discover that I can get out of almost any unpleasant school assignment other than math or wood shop by merely offering to write a five- or ten-

or twenty-page paper on the topic. I never seriously heed a teacher's syllabus again.[2]

I veered away from Arnold by the time high school arrived, his outsiderness reaching regular truancy. With my home life, school presented itself as an alternate society (if not reality), an utter necessity. Arnold got a job after school working for the local hospital, but rumor had it that he'd been fired for taking an amputated arm home instead of following proper procedures for its disposal. Soon after, he joined the military. Some time later, the *Albany Times* noted that he was a part of the honor guard at some major state function, perhaps Johnson's 1965 inauguration. Once in the very early '70s, I ran into him wearing full leather biker drag in Moe's Books in Berkeley. When I saw him at State nearly 20 years later (it was he who recognized me), the narrative of clothing was aging beach boy, his torso and limbs, every visible inch, covered with tattoos. He had come to study writing.

The "average" sentence in *Albany* is 6.94 words long.

My father withheld child support, forcing my mother to live with her parents, my brother and I to be raised together in a small room.

At night we would lie in our two single beds across from one another and I would tell Cliff, two years, seven months younger, long stories, the sort of gothic horror only a nine-year-old could envision. He would tell me to stop and start to whimper and finally begin crying so that eventually my mother would burst in to tell us to be quiet. This went on for years, until I was old enough to get a crystal radio set and flashlight, and could hide under the covers, listening to the all-news station and reading Steinbeck novels until I fell asleep.

The cruelty of my behavior is evident. It's not an excuse to say that I was nine years old, or twelve. What motivated me? Over forty years later, it is still unclear to me whether I was driven out of a confused sense that my brother's arrival shortly after the disappearance of my father had been, in some vague way, the cause of that man's abandonment, or whether the practice of emotional terrorism (modeled with such artistry by my grandmother) was simply the only form of autonomy I understood.

Grandfather called them niggers.

So that I was surprised at how many elderly African American men, all, like my grandfather, members of the Veterans for Foreign Wars (VFW), came to his funeral.

I can't afford an automobile.

At first, the long ride out on the bus from San Francisco to San Rafael was a luxury. Prohibited by Selective Service regulation from earning a living wage at my Conscientious Objector's "alternative service" job, I worked for the Committee for Prisoner Humanity & Justice (CPHJ) for the first year at no salary, the second year at just $125 per month. To survive, I found a part-time night job doing layout and paste-up with the *Kalendar*, a first-generation gay bar newspaper whose editor and publisher harbored dim fantasies of developing an empire of alternative media if he could just meet this week's payroll. With barely enough money to afford my $50-per-month rent in a large communal flat opposite the Panhandle in the Haight, I often hitchhiked the seventeen miles north over the Golden Gate Bridge to work and back. Later, as funds became more plentiful and my need to be reasonably on time grew, I chose to ride the Golden Gate Transit buses[3] out, hitching back in the evening rush.

The Golden Gate system was notably different from both the San Francisco Municipal Railway (the "Muni") or my earlier experiences with AC Transit in the East Bay. I would board the bus on Van Ness and after only a couple more stops in San Francisco, the bus tended only to lose passengers as it traveled north through Marin County. This meant that if I picked my seating with a little luck and care, I could sit without a rider next to me for the entire 30-minute ride, an unusually smooth journey given the state of the then-new buses and the fact that our journey was against commute traffic on the freeway. If other transit systems were carnivals of human interaction, filled with the racial and class conflicts that find themselves funneled into public space, the Golden Gate buses were a refuge. Often the bus was quieter and more private than my home. I would read or stare out the window and increasingly I began to use the time in order to write.[4]

**Far across the calm bay stood a complex of long yellow
buildings, a prison.**

Because the hill sloped away from the rear of the house, the
modest five-step red cement front porch was counterbal-
anced by a long rickety wooden stairway leading down to
the yard in the rear. There was room enough at the top of
that splintery deck for no more than one adult to stand (the
only one who ever did, really, was my grandmother, reaching into the clothespin bin that my grandfather must have
built into the railing, hanging clothes on a line nearly
twenty feet over the yard). I would spend hours up there,
looking out over the minuscule expanse that was our back-
yard, with its lone tree next to our small sway-back garage, a
hydrangea bush in the near corner, a few straggles of berry
bushes against the chain-link fence that separated our yard
from that of an old woman who lived by herself on the next
block over. On a clear day, I could see beyond Albany Hill all
the way across the bay to Mount Tamalpais and, further to
the north, right at the water's edge San Quentin. Who did I
think lived there? Doing what?

My grandfather's one real friend from the Pabco plant,
Virgil Garcia, was jailed for vehicular manslaughter and
sent to "Tamal."[5] One summer day, my grandparents, my
brother and I rode the Richmond-San Rafael ferry—we were
headed for a week's vacation along the Russian River—and
stopped in the parking lot of the prison. My grandfather got
out of the pale '51 Pontiac and walked up to and eventually
through the entrance of the medieval-looking structure,
disappearing inside for a visit that lasted at least an hour
while the rest of us waited in the summer sun. What did I
think this meant?

Who was Virgil Garcia? He was a figure of conversation from time to time at home, but as was true for everyone but immediate relatives and a few members of my grandmother's VFW Ladies Auxiliary branch, he never set foot in our house. I never once saw the man. Having served his term, Garcia returned to his job in Emeryville, retiring a year ahead of my grandfather. Within a week of his retirement party, Garcia committed suicide.

A line is the distance between.

I'm waiting in a long queue to register for classes at San Francisco State. The fellow in front of me, wiry and lively-eyed David Perry, turns out to be a writing major likewise, a grad student by way of Bard. I quickly blurt (brag?) that I'm "in correspondence" with Robert Kelly, with whom he's studied. It turns out that there are other Kelly students in the area, at Berkeley—Harvey Bialy, a microbiologist/poet married to a slender, intense exotic dancer named Timotha, and John Gorham, a graduate student in English and possibly the finest natural lyric poet I would ever meet.

Bialy is giving a reading soon thereafter in Albany in the same two-room public library where, just three years earlier, I'd first discovered Williams' *The Desert Music* and seen in an instant how poetry could be put to non-narrative purposes. Bialy's poetry is spare and intellectual in a way that doesn't tell me anything other than that it wants to be known as such. I much prefer Bialy's reading mate, a Canadian graduate student at Berkeley named David Bromige. Paul Mariah, a poet I've known slightly through the open readings at the Rambam Bookstore in Berkeley, does the introductions.

To get home afterwards, I thumb a ride. A car stops immediately, the driver a slightly older fellow—he's 29, I'm 21—I'd
seen in the back of the crowd at the reading. In the time it
takes him to drive me back to my apartment in the Adams
Point neighborhood of Oakland (I don't realize for some
time just how far out of his way he has gone), we discover
not only an affinity to the poetics of Bromige, but that we
shared a strong sense of Robert Duncan's importance, an
interest in Zukofsky and Ashbery, and even a friend, one of
my early publishers, Iven Lourie of the *Chicago Review*, having
been the driver's roommate for a time back at the University
of Chicago. The driver introduces himself as David Melnick,
and he turns out to be a shy, witty, brilliant person, deeply
insecure. One of the three most intelligent people I will ever
meet, we instantly become friends for life.

Through these people (especially Melnick and Gorham and
Bromige) I will gradually get to know first hand a much
broader community, including Ken Irby, Tom Meyer,
Jonathan Williams, Sherril Jaffe, Jack Shoemaker, David
Sandberg, d alexander, Joanne Kyger, and Jerome
Rothenberg. These poets are, with only the exceptions of
Perry and Gorham, older, more confident, more widely
published. There are only a couple with whom I feel
comfortable enough even to speak as a possible equal.
(Melnick and Bromige, democrats both, pretend not to
notice, coaxing me, prodding.)

Beyond Ashbery, Zukofsky and Duncan, Melnick's favorite
poet is David Shapiro, whose early success with trade
publishers intimidates me. I also don't know how to take the
casual sense of form practiced by the New York School in
general. I'm reading Olson's *Maximus* poems, all of

Blackburn, anything I can get by Whalen, Duncan's *Passages* as they appear. I'm still trying to figure out how to write The Poem. I still envision it as a distinct formed object, perfect for publication in a magazine.

In 1968, the problem of form is the problem of the line. It, I decide, is the question that nobody, not even Olson, knows how to answer.[6] What, in free verse, does it mean? Olson's answer, more rigorous and less mushily metaphysical than Williams', is nonetheless filled with gaps and contradictions. Yet even an O'Hara and a Ginsberg seem to acknowledge it. Without ever having read a word of Derrida, I distrust the essentialism of speech Olson's projective verse appears to propose (later I will realize that I've turned Olson's poetry into a straw man, his position in my head far more extreme than any he ever took in life, and only after that, a good while after that, will I come to recognize how useful this process had been).

By 1969, I'm also reading modernist fiction. In a notebook, I try over and over to craft out a "perfect paragraph," with the opening sentence of Faulkner's *Sound and the Fury* as my model. The only part that will survive is "the garbage barge at the bridge." The origin of the sentence in my work is a reaction to the Faulkner, to the Joyce of *Ulysses*, the Kerouac of *Visions of Cody*, Stein everywhere. I sit on the roof of an apartment house now at the edge of the Rad Lab woods just north of the UC campus, watching the sun set into the high-rises of San Francisco, reworking the passage endlessly. One model in my mind, at some point, was Ponge's *Notebook of the Pine Woods*, a journal of the author's stay in hiding from the Nazis during which he attempts a single sonnet. Writing and rewriting my paragraph, I escape any concern that I'm merely imitating Creeley, Olson, Williams, Duncan, Kelly or Eshleman in this poem or that. It also allows me a strategy for literature without progress. I use everything I ever learned about the line, but without ever having to decide what precisely this was. It will be another five years before I actually start to write poetry in prose.

The "problem" with the line may be, ultimately, that there is no problem.

They circled the seafood restaurant, singing "We shall not be moved."

By the time I was a senior in high school, I was already participating in the picket lines of the Congress of Racial Equality, mostly at Jack London Square in downtown Oakland, careful not to tell my mother or grandparents where I was going. I knew hardly anyone—they were all college age and older and seemed infinitely more worldly— but I wanted to know them all—that may have been the point—but I was too timid to speak to anyone beyond the singing and chanting that ran as a constant soundtrack to these events. These were the first interracial crowds in which I'd ever found myself. They represented some utopian possibility, a voluntary association that existed solely through action and driven by desire and honor and a sense of justice. The contrast with my family, claustrophobic and seethingly dysfunctional as it was, could not have been more striking.

At some of these pickets in early '65, I began to notice one woman, a few years older than myself, with thick black bangs, intense brown eyes and a sharp, ready laugh, a natural leader. She was one of the very few people who would make eye contact with me and one day at an afternoon demonstration at Spenger's in Berkeley I recall her coming up to me to ask why people seemed so upset. "Malcom X was murdered this morning," I replied. This was how I first spoke with Rochelle Nameroff, who would become my first wife.

My turn to cook.

In the 1960s, mixed vegetables stir-fried in a wok, tossed over brown rice.

In the '90s, poached salmon, just barely cooked. Broccoli, steamed but still crisp. Couscous, which few people seem to realize is actually a pasta, the world's oldest.

It was hard to adjust my sleeping to those hours when the sun was up.

The buses had not yet begun running when my shift was over, so I walked up Main Street from Paul's Pies, then over toward our apartment at the edge of the park. How was I going to do this when winter arrived, with the lake effect snow that invariably hit Buffalo? The entrance to our apartment was up the rear stairs and we couldn't afford real curtains so there was no way to keep the sun out as I tossed and turned and tried to sleep.

The event was nothing like their report of it.

Working all day as a shipping clerk for PG&E in Emeryville, I was unable to get to the UC administrative building in which the students were holding their sit-in before the campus police locked the building at 5 p.m. For hours, I and several thousand other people milled around the building, singing songs from the civil rights movement along with the several hundred students indoors. People brought newly purchased plastic garbage cans filled with hot coffee, plus small buckets filled with birth control pills for the women now locked in. These were sent up ropes to the second floor balconies while film crews in the building's lobby turned their kliegs on us. The entire plaza had the air of a festival about it, with the very serious undertext of the presence of the police.

I stayed until midnight, then headed home as I had another long day at work the following morning, so was not around when, at 4:00 a.m., Governor Pat Brown (at the urging of local officials who claimed that the offices were being trashed by demonstrators, which was not true) sent in the cops and over 450 students were arrested.

The next evening, Brown was quoted by Walter Cronkite on the CBS Evening News as declaring that students had been misled by outside agitators. To illustrate the concept, the screen showed the images of us on the building's steps outside, carefully raising buckets and cans up the ladders. I was on screen for all of five seconds.

The following morning, when I reported for work, I was told that my position as stock clerk was "no longer needed."

How concerned was I over her failure to have orgasms?

She asked Rochelle if it was okay to fuck me before she asked me. The first time we made love it took 30 minutes to locate her diaphragm, then the bed collapsed (at which point, and not before, we realized one of her roommates had nudged open the door and was watching, one hand in his trousers). The first time she attempted oral sex, she vomited. To an 18 year old, someone in their mid-20s seems "in command." My own repertoire at that age went from A to B. At first it must have seemed like a solution, yet very quickly her thrashing and awkwardness, her anger and frustration became deeper addictions. Years later, when, after much uncertainty and back-and-forth, she concluded she really was a lesbian, she said to me, "When I decided to give up men, you seemed like a good place to start."

What was I thinking of? She was an intelligent young woman, courageous in her life choices, whose one mistake was to imagine that the most direct road to what she might want led through the beds of those who possessed whatever might be the immediate object of desire. I failed or refused to understand what my own motives were. At first it was pure pleasure combined with cowardice: I was unable to extricate myself from a marriage that had ended emotionally a year or more earlier without an alternate relationship at hand. The idea of being single gave me vertigo. Later, when it had become clear what her interest was and its limits, I refused to acknowledge them either. It was not a matter of being "out of control"—I had no clue as to what "control" might entail.

Mondale's speech was drowned by jeers.

Dianne Feinstein, recognizing that her chances of being nominated as his running mate were fading in front her eyes, leaned into the microphone and scolded the crowd at Justin Herman Plaza, which only booed more vigorously.

Ye wretched.

The smallest fragment of song, if it is the right song, can ignite what Proust rightly called the involuntary memory. *The Internationale* will ring in my ears as coins are being placed upon my eyes. In much the same way as my grand-mother always broke down weeping whenever she heard a solo bugle play *Taps*. Similarly, the receptors in my body cued for acid and speed reawaken now decades later at any tune from *Highway 61 Revisited*. When Peggy Jeffries left, virtually without warning, for India in 1975, I realized that playing the music of Marvin Gaye over and over might provide short term solace, but would ultimately make it impossible for me to listen to that music in the future. And it has.

She introduces herself as a rape survivor.

Everyone has a story and some are worse than others. In her instance, it had been violent. She may have been sodomized with a gun. After a period in which she lived on the streets and then joined an ashram and donated her belongings to her guru, she showed up on the other coast, becoming active in women's issues, but she found it increasingly difficult to work in groups.

Yet his best friend was Hispanic.

What I know of my grandfather's family is almost entirely hearsay, although I never once in the 15 years I lived with the man heard him speak of them. His mother was "a monster," "a terror," "cold" and "mean." On that my mother and grandmother both agreed.(I should be suspicious. This is the exact story I hear about my father and his family from my maternal grandmother.) His own father, grandson of the British naval explorer Sir John Franklin, had been killed by a car on Thanksgiving Day sometime around 1910. One brother moved to Lodi, a farm town in the central valley, changing his first name to Frank to the bafflement of all. Another, Charles Tansley, stayed in the Berkeley area, but the only times I ever saw him was at a small service station on Monterey where he would sit on an overturned drum spitting into the grease, trading lies with his friends.[7] There was a sister whom I never recall having met.

My grandmother's first memory of him came from an event in the combined fifth-sixth grade class at LeConte School they attended. A fellow student had had a seizure and my grandfather, following the recommended practice of the day, had inserted his belt into the boy's mouth to keep him from swallowing his tongue. While my grandmother, the youngest of 11 surviving children in a single-parent household, only made it to ninth grade, my grandfather graduated from Oakland Technical High School and worked briefly for Santa Fe railroad before joining the army and shipping off to Paris to load taxis with munitions during the First World War. Returning, he took a job with what was then called the Paraffin Company in Emeryville where he worked from 1919 until 1961.

Aside from Virgil Garcia, they had no apparent friends other than the chapter members of the Berkeley Veterans of Foreign Wars which, in the 1950s and '60s, actively supported the work of the House Un-American Activities Committee. In retrospect this seems odd, given their consistent support of the Democratic Party and rather intense dislike of Richard Nixon. In a house in which there were virtually no books other than *Readers Digest* condensed novels, my grandfather was a news junky. He read the *Oakland Tribune* end to end every evening, watched John Cameron Swazee and later Huntley and Brinkley with a predictability Spinoza would have understood, riding around with the car radio invariably turned to news. It was his bulky black Royal typewriter, purchased in order to carry out his duties in the VFW, which, in my later years in high school, I would carry from its perch on a small table in the dining room and set up in the kitchen, typing away novels, school papers and my first attempts at poetry.

He taught me how to bat, taking me to Bushrod Field in North Oakland where he'd first learned to play. When it came time, in my teen years, to teach me how to tie a tie, he did so grudgingly. Our relationship was already strained and ties were, for him, something he wore only a few days each year. He tried once or twice to teach me how to drive, but began shouting whenever I made a mistake.

I decided not to escape to Canada.

Functionally, I was an idiot, appealing my draft status without benefit of a lawyer. In 1964, when I first registered and applied for Conscientious Objector's status, the standard measurement was a demonstrable family commitment to pacifism within clearly defined religious framework. I was the son of an ex-cop and navy veteran with a bad (and documented) habit of assaulting people and the guys on this board *knew him*. I cited passages of Kerouac and mumbled some argument about an indigenous mode of Zen Buddhism. My rejection reached appeal sometime around 1967 and the board examiner wrote mostly about my showing up to the hearing in a surplus-store Army jacket. I may have been the only person ever denied for reasons of style.

Showing the file to a draft counselor at UC Berkeley, he got on the phone to Ann Fagan Ginger, a lawyer who ran the Meiklejohn Civil Liberties Institute, an anti-draft legal assistance project, out of her garage in Berkeley. Later that same day, she read the files as I sat silently in front of her and, without even asking me, picked up the phone and called the ACLU.

Revenue enhancement.

I do not recall a time in which I was not the absolutely poorest kid in my class.

Competition and spectacle, kinds of drugs.

In the early 1970s, the *Poetry Project Newsletter* would dutifully list all of the contributors to current magazines except for except for myself, Watten, Andrews and a few others the editor felt certain were part of this bad new nameless thing.

In 1978, the Art Institute auditorium, as Barrett began to draw an analogy between Zukofsky's poetry and a scientific concept, Robert Duncan, who had already finished speaking, went ballistic, leaping up, flapping his arms like a crow, yelling, "No, no, no. Zukofsky was all about life, all about song"—a conception of song that would have made any 20th century composer cringe (and which, at least at that early moment, Watten had never denied). If this was to be an Oedipal moment, Duncan understood the role assigned to him and so determined to slay the threat before it did him.

What Tom Clark objected to most was not our poetics, but the simple fact that, insofar as we did not fit any of the previous aesthetic buckets, we changed an invisible internal balance of the larger whole, and it was that whole to which he had committed his life, his desire, his imagination.

If it demonstrates form some people won't read it.

Form proposes its telos: "I know just how many lines this sonnet will take." In 1981, when I wrote "Albany," there was still significant controversy over the deliberately "inorganic" elements of my poetry, especially the use of repetition in *Ketjak* and the Fibonacci number system in *Tjanting*. Poetic fashion has changed and changed again since then, and it most certainly will continue to do so.

Was I "betraying" my literary ancestors (and in what sense did I admit their paternity)? In a sense that both Olson and Duncan would have understood, it has all always been one poem. This one, to be exact:

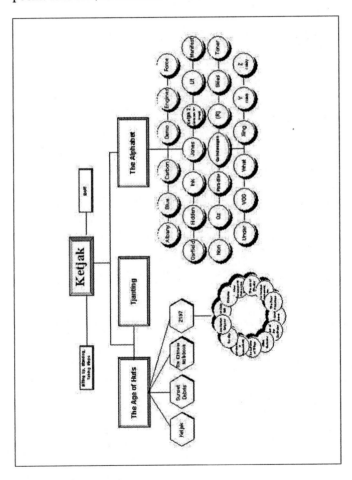

When I look at this chart, which I've been using for several years now,[8] what it tells me is that to work, to maintain the sense of balance that seems to govern my intuition of what goes where and to what degree, is first of all a sense of the size and scope of the next level of the work: it must roughly equal all that has gone before. Roughly is a very general term: *The Alphabet* is nearly twice the length of all the other works on this chart. Combined.

What the chart doesn't show is how, or when, or why, there has been a shift in the work from structures that carried forward a formal concept as a mechanism for breaking up the habits of perception and those that tend to define a form and in the process to seek mechanisms of sub- and diversion. It begins in *The Alphabet* very early. I can find its traces already in the first section I ever wrote for *The Alphabet*, "Force," written a year before *Albany*.

In fact, far from being the apotheosis of exoskeletal determinism in poetry, as I've sometimes been portrayed, I find that I've spent 17 of the last 24 years actively undercutting expectations within form, compared with the seven year stretch that begins with *Ketjak* and proceeds through *Tjanting*.

This thought makes me wonder if I shouldn't think now of proceeding in yet another way.

Television unifies conversation.

Our next door neighbors, the Pruters, were the first ones on the block to own a set, a large box with a small blue round screen. A year later, when we first bought ours, we would turn it on at 5:00 p.m. every day, letting it warm up for a half hour against one of the test patterns that was on before the arrival of the first broadcast, *Howdy Doody*.

Died in action.

Chris Martinez is a superb infielder and your basically happy kid. His house, right on the corner of Nielson and Marin, is covered with foliage, as if vegetation would protect the family from the fast, heavy traffic of Marin. We play pickup games of baseball in the elementary school playground hour after hour. Whenever Chris plays, I shift to the outfield, because he's the better second baseman. He and his best friend, Ray Nottingham, always show up and leave together. They are in our minds a unit. Since they are both one year younger, I don't see them socially once we get past the age of pickup hardball.

Later, Ray's dad sits on the local Selective Service board and takes the role of my inquisitor. Do I think all violence is bad? What would I do if I discovered Adolph Hitler attacking my mother? The two other panel members, one on either side, stare at me, silent. I am terrified of them. This panel is my nightmare of older male authority. I feel powerless and threatened.

Decades later, on the wall in the mall in Washington, it only takes a few minutes to find Chris' name.

If a man is a player, he will have no job.

Around were not a few, but dozens of young writers who seemed content to work at the most minimal part-time positions in order to free up time to write. I was always showing up at readings late and exhausted, having just gotten in off a bus from Sacramento or San Rafael. I never "couldn't find the time to write."

Becoming prepared to live with less space.

After nearly three years during which I'd had only one roommate at a time, I wanted a larger number of people to bounce off of, less of the immediate competition one got (I got) over the tightly rationed physical resources of a flat. I also was worried about money. Rents in San Francisco had risen much faster than my ability to earn a living in the prison movement.

At a natural food store on Clement, I saw an add for a room in a seven bedroom house on California, right at the edge of Pacific Heights. The people, all of whom were younger than I, seemed friendly, intelligent, straight forward. I was pleased that there had been no turnover in the apartment in the preceding two years. But a gay man, filmmaker Artie Bresnan, had just moved out after the one couple in the house had given birth to a young boy, Alyosha. What I didn't realize at the time (although possibly I should have) was what a transformative, even explosive event that child was to "communal" life.

My room was to be a closed-in back porch, no more than 12 by 12, but it opened onto a large, almost cavernous room that I was told I could make my own, but had to leave open as it was the sole "public" pathway to the downstairs john. I painted the room a deep yellow, almost a goldenrod, and Elliot Helfer, a roommate of mine from a few years before, contributed some furniture—a dining room table and Morris chair that he had built himself. I set up bricks and boards in the yellow room and mounted the first truly serious bookcase I'd ever managed.

The day I moved in, one of my new roommates wandered about the downstairs naked all afternoon (I think this was a test). She was getting ready to go to Stanford, which had already accepted her, but before she'd moved into the house on California Street, she'd been in the county jail for boosting checkbooks and credit cards from people's mailboxes. At the time I knew her, she was a bartender in the Tenderloin (although, still working in the prison movement, I didn't yet know what that might involve).

Her boyfriend carried a sullen macho act to an extreme. One night, sitting on the front porch, she sighed that she wished that streetlamp wasn't glaring down at them. He took a pistol out and shot the light out. The bullet ricocheted through the room in which Alyosha and his parents were trying to sleep. Their reaction was to move.

It rapidly became evident that this beautiful and entirely harmless infant had set off a chain of events and, within six weeks, I found myself the last remaining member of the household. I called the lady, an ill-tempered, horrible German woman who lived in the Sunset, and arranged to take over responsibility for 3028 California Street. I then put signs—3 by 5 cards really—up at the San Francisco Art Institute and in the laundromats, bookstores and natural food stores in town.

My idea was that I would pick the first of my six new room-mates, then she or he and I would then pick the second one, then the three of us the next, and so on until we had filled the house. Because of my finances, I needed to accomplish this quickly. I couldn't afford more than a single month of the rent for the entire seven bedroom home—$350. But I couldn't decide who, precisely, should be that critical first roommate. One fellow I liked a lot was a tall, laconic paint-ing student at the Art Institute, Mel Laubach. Another was a hippie nurse by the name of Peggy Jeffries. Finally, almost at the last moment (both had virtually given up on me), I settled on Mel and persuaded him to interview Peggy. She had only a day left in her flat in the Mission when we called to invite her to join us. The next person to join us were Richie Jenkins, a country rock guitarist who'd once played in a band at Queens College called the Bankers, fronted by lead singer Lorenzo Thomas.[9] He was followed by a grad student at San Francisco State who was studying for a special ed teaching certificate, Liz Montague. We then picked on an extraordinarily quiet and shy nutritionist and a tiny young woman who was a hotwalk at a local racetrack.

Having arrived at six, we were unable to agree on the final person. We'd interviewed maybe 50 people over two weeks and everybody was tired and exhausted and disgusted. None of the people we'd met had been able to muster up more than two positive votes for admission. It looked bleak and we held a house meeting one evening (we were waiting for the 51st interviewing victim to arrive). Instead of looking for what we wanted in an ideal roommate we concluded, we should instead identify in advance what we *didn't* want. Even here we found ourselves hopelessly vague. All we could agree on was that we didn't want a rock drummer—that would be just hopelessly noisy.

Soon after, the doorbell rang and in walked Frank India. He was, he explained, a rock drummer. He laughed when we explained our collective (and massive) groan, and described how drummers used practice pads. We took it as a sign and he moved in almost immediately. This combination of roommates lasted without change for maybe 18 months.

As I had to catch the bus 17 miles out to CPHJ in San Rafael every morning (except for the days I had to catch a Greyhound 90 miles to Sacramento), I was the early riser in the group. Since Peggy usually worked the night shift, first at Children's Hospital (six blocks west of the house) and later at Mount Zion (six blocks east), we'd often pass at the kitchen table. We had long quiet conversations every morning for months and I gradually got so I couldn't hear the thick Carolina accent any more.

This house turned out to be the perfect collective living situation. We'd all spontaneously troop over to the local ice cream parlor after dinner, a virtual party in motion, or else all catch the bus (none of us owned a car) down to Chinatown to catch a double bill for 99 cents at the Times Theater, or possibly to see the Cockettes. Richie's band played down off of Union Street and had a single forthcoming from Fantasy Records. Lizzie decided to translate some of *Ketjak* into American Sign Language for a class she was taking, and Mel decided to turn this into a performance for one of his classes, held in this instance at the downtown Museum of Modern Art on Van Ness.

It was the kind of house where I could bring home a rotting bear rug that I'd found literally in a dumpster around the corner and put it into the middle of the living room floor and everybody declared they loved it, so that it stayed for months, even though you could smell the faint, sweet odor of mold.

We also had great parties, with everyone taking seriously the lone rule that you had to invite at least 12 people each. Beer and grass and red wine and amyl nitrate flowed freely. At one party, a well known poet fell down the back stairs while trying to fuck a coke dealing literary wanna-be. Everyone thought of it as *style*.

My one sexual relationship at the time I first moved to California Street was a casual affair I'd been having with a married friend. Casual in the sense that it had no narrative —it was literally, and by design, not going anywhere. It was a relationship I'd begun in college when I was still married to Shelly, who had first introduced us. Off and on, it continued on a sexual level for over a decade. A brilliant artist in her own right, this woman was/is, more than anything, a dear friend, which gave our sex a sense of play (and occasionally even incestuousness). We never planned anything. The sex was spontaneous and the situation carried its own sense of risk. Never once did she lead me to believe that she ever intended to leave her husband, whom she clearly loved. What she was looking for in this has never been clear to me, especially when she got involved with other people, both men and women. What I seemed to be looking for, and this is hindsight, was to understand the infinite depths of friendship. We would have long, casual discussions about everything in the world, her own edge-of-lumpen origins a perspective remarkably close to my own. Next to David Melnick, she was the second person in my life to see and unconditionally accept me for who I was, a gift that I think may be the most difficult to give.[10]

The only one of my roommates who ever openly disapproved of this arrangement was Peggy, who at the time declared that she was attempting to swear off men and sex altogether, attending meetings of followers of the original "Don't Worry, Be Happy" guru, Meher Baba. Peg told me, in a nonaccusative way, that I was involved because the sex was safe. Nobody was asking for any sort of commitment from me and the highly variable nature of the relationship (we could go for months between assignations) didn't get in the way of my work.

One night everyone in the house, plus a few folks who more or less happened to sitting around the kitchen table, decided to head over to a restaurant on 24th Street. Over dinner, we agreed to head back across town to the Presidio Theatre, which was then showing the Erotic Film Festival. The films were all shorts, mostly student work, only a small portion of which could ever have been called hardcore porn. One consisted entirely of a person eating slices of an orange in extreme close-up.

After the films, Peggy brought one of the guests (a poet and friend of mine) back home and everyone in the house could hear them groaning and gasping in her room upstairs for hours. I realized that her "anti-sex" rap had its limits, or at least its exceptions. Even more important, I felt crushed. It made me realize that I had begun to think of her as something other (and more) than "just a roommate."

Some weeks later, after a long Saturday on which Elliot Helfer and I had gone hiking in Tilden only to get lost amid a dense forest of brambles, I had to rush to the First Unitarian Church as CPHJ was holding a film benefit on which I'd promised to work. As I was heading through the kitchen on my way out, Peggy said that she wanted to see the movie, an ancient black-and-white chain-gang classic. She grabber her purse and came along. Afterwards, we took the 38 Geary back, walking the last half mile down Presidio to California, when I leaned over and kissed her. This led to a series of questions that lasted off and on for two days. What was I looking for? Would I be willing to take responsibility for birth control? Was I going to try and change her spirituality?

I must have answered adequately, since late one evening the following week, when I'd found myself nodding off during conversation in the living room with the rest of the gang and had excused myself and gone to bed, Peggy came into my room, slipped out of her jeans, climbing under the covers. "Okay. Here I am," she said.

Nora the nutritionist had seen Peggy slip into my room, not to return. By the time we got up the following morning, the entire house knew what had happened. There was a lot of eye-rolling and a few jokes in modestly bad taste. At least a couple of people were upset—one woman who'd decided that she was going to seduce me and the live-in (non-rent paying) beau of one of the other women who viewed Peg with more than a little interest—although it would be weeks before we would figure this out.

For a couple of months, life seemed perfect. I was in the middle of writing *The Age of Huts* and felt my poetry was really breaking into new territory. Every time I opened the notebook I got excited. Barrett Watten had promised to bring *Ketjak* as a book out soon. It was gradually becoming evident that California would soon pass a bill eliminating the indeterminate sentence, the only question was when and with what kind of terms to replace it (I was hard at work answering that latter question). Living in a large collective household with my lover seemed like just the right balance of privacy and intimacy.

One evening I was standing in the living room talking with Richie. In the kitchen, I could hear Peggy talking with Mel. I hear her say, "I've decided I'm moving to India and I think I'm going to stay." It was the first I'd even heard of this idea, but (as I wander in dumbfounded to the next room) she's already bought the ticket. Six weeks later, she's gone.

As it happened, she didn't stay forever, but by the time she returned, I'd given up and was seeing other women. We tried, off and on for the next three years, to re-establish the spark our affair had had those first few months, but one of us was always desperately seeking out the other, whose head was for the moment someplace else. It devolved into an adolescent break-up and make-up pattern.

In late 1977, she'd gone back to North Carolina for a few months when the members of the household (which had gone through an almost complete recycling of roommates after Peg departed for India) voted to go on rent strike as the landlord refused to do repairs. The landlord sued and people began abandoning the house for better quarters. I moved to Tom Mandel's flat in the Haight and put Peg's stuff into cartons in his garage. When she returned, we took over Kit Robinson's old apartment on San Jose Avenue and tried living together as a couple. After six months, we both knew it wasn't working. She moved out and eventually returned to the Carolinas.

Live ammunition.

The windows of the Main Library seemed to implode and the small "bookmobile" by the entrance rocked as its walls freckled with gunshot. We'd locked the door of our second-floor classroom in Wheeler, but were unable to keep ourselves from peeking out the window in horror as the deputy sheriff raised a shotgun and fired into the Rare Books Room across the path. Nobody said a word.

Secondary boycott.

By the mid-1980s, the political activists I hang out with are beginning to confront the same set of questions facing my poet friends—how, in one's mid-life to move from transitory inadequate jobs to some sense of continuity as a life, which means a sense of career that may (or may not) be related directly to writing or activism. In the DSA office, national political director Jim Shoch complains that it's impossible to have an "interesting" conversation with members of this same organization Jim has spent 15 years building. He's already applied to graduate school.

My crime is parole violation.

The joint has a discourse and logic that took years to learn. There are a variety of ways people can avoid telling you what exactly they've done to warrant incarceration. Even harder for an outsider to fathom is the sense of time as urgency without future. The sense was not the continuous present of modernism, but rather a perpetual one in which every moment was new, in formation. This proved ultimately to be more important lesson than anything I had learned in college. Twenty-one years after leaving CPHJ, it still governs the function of time in my writing.

Now that the piecards have control.

What was the moment in which any hope for the left's ability to form a majority coalition that could genuinely govern in the US was truly lost? Was it as late as 1968? Or did it occur earlier? When the labor movement broke off from socialism? When unions stopped being activist and became service organizations?

Rubin feared McClure would read *Ghost Tantras* at the teach-in.

Jerry Rubin was, I immediately surmised, a jerk. But this woman who was volunteering as his secretary was not. With her dark bangs, long flowing hair, intense brown eyes and sharp, almost explosive laugh, she was entirely unlike anyone I'd ever met in my waspy world before. I was apparently the only person they'd found who had any idea how to contact Dave Van Ronk (and my thought was merely to phone Izzy Young at Folk City in New York), but this made me a sort of resource. Shortly thereafter, I ran into her again at Pepe's, the pizza parlor of choice for Telegraph Avenue street people in 1965. She was hunting for a mutual friend in search of some grass. I was reading either *Naked Lunch* or *Last Exit to Brooklyn* and it occurred to her that I was literary. She asked me what I knew of Yeats, but, knowing nothing, I was derisive. She'd just come from the opening performance of the film *Help*, which she gushed over. Since I considered the Beatles a commercial rip-off, I was even more derisive. She challenged me to see the film with her the next day, which I did, interpreting it as a series of psychedelic drug jokes. Had she ever taken acid? She had not. So the following night we saw the film again (skipping the second feature, Glenn Ford or someone like that in *The Love Boat*), stopping at the drinking fountain on the way in to wash down some commercially produced Sandoz. After the film was over, she went into the women's restroom and didn't return for nearly an hour. She'd been, she told me, watching the walls. Over the course of the next week I also introduced her to DMT, which at the moment was a friend and I were trying without great success to introduce into the Berkeley market. It had few of the psychological effects associated with acid and lasted for only a very brief period, less than an hour, but the visual hallucinations were far more intense and one felt as if one's limbs had been rendered into some soft and pliable material.

One night after a party, we returned to Rubin's office above some stores at the corner of Telegraph and Dwight, where the organizing committee permitted her to sleep. On Rubin's couch in that dark office, I lost my virginity to Rochelle Nameroff who, on Halloween just two months later, I would marry.

This form is the study group.

College is a process that takes bright young people and renders them illiterate. None more so than the professors who are forced to remain within the confines of this institution, replicating the cycle over and over. My teachers at Berkeley, at San Francisco State, at Merritt College had perfect contempt for one another and none of them—with the exceptions of Bob Grenier and Ed van Aelstyn (one of the founders of *Coyote's Journal* who briefly taught linguistics at SF State)—could have ever read the work of someone such as Jackson Mac Low.

For me, very early on, perhaps because I was publishing and going to readings and giving readings before I really went to college, the community of the poem, of the reading scenes and small presses, with always that concentrating, centering fact of the text, any text, at hand, in front of one's eyes, words forming in the mind from the muteness of letters clustered alone invisible lines—the community of the poem was (and remains) the center around which learning in my life can occur.

I dedicate poems precisely because I want to invoke this community, to say its real name(s).

The sparts are impeccable, though filled with deceit.

The long crowd milled into the auditorium to hear the panel and its lead speaker, the head of the FMLN, while outside members of the Sparticist League not only waved banners denouncing him as a traitor to the left, but brought their own spotlights in hopes of attracting some TV time.

As early as high school, Trotskyism had been attractive to me because it was the only tendency visible on the Left (I knew nothing at the time of the Frankfurt School) that always articulated, at once, both the value of Marxist analysis and the horrific depredations that were Stalinism. Any history of the United States in the Twentieth Century that does not attempt to comprehend the trajectory and fate of the various Trot tendencies is useless.

A benefit reading.

I had never put on a reading before, but thought I could get Bob Creeley, then living in Bolinas, Joanne Kyger (ditto), and Edward Dorn, who was staying that year in the Sunset District, to agree. I sent each a letter, explaining what CPHJ was, its relation to the California prison movement, the movement's general direction, what the location for the reading was like (the First Unitarian Church on Franklin in San Francisco), etc. My co-workers were supportive, but probably more bemused than anything—why rent such a large room for a poetry reading? Who were *these* people (none of my co-workers had ever heard of any of them)? Before I could even follow up with phone calls, Dorn called and asked me to come see him. I left work early, hitched (my characteristic mode of transportation in the 1970s) down to the City and caught a bus out past Golden Gate Park and took the long walk uphill to a small white stucco dwelling on a block crammed with little single family homes (the walls, like so much of San Francisco, nearly touching). Dorn's house was chaotic, an ironing board dominating the middle of the living room, his wife and a young woman who was introduced cursorily as "the nanny" chasing after kids. "Nobody told me about the fog in the summer out here," he said, waving me over to a round dining room table. "The idea of 12 months of indoor behavior is intolerable." He wanted to know in great detail about the CPHJ (Creeley and Kyger both later agreed without a single question about the group or its work or the movement in general), how was it funded, did we serve all kinds of prisoners and not just the media "stars," what was San Quentin like, what was my relation to the group, etc. As we talked he reached into an open bowl on the table and began to roll a joint the size of a small cigar. He passed it over and I took a deep first breath, my lungs and throat clinching tight to avoid coughing. It was harsh weed, the strongest I had ever smoked. Dorn finally had one condition, that he be allowed to go on last so that he could arrive at the last moment and not have to deal with either Creeley or Kyger. I agreed, which was how it finally occurred.

On the night of the event itself, during the intermission, Opal Nations, new at the time to the United States, came up to say that he had never been at a reading with 400 people before. I had, but I certainly had never tried to set something up like that. It had been (in retrospect) remarkably easy.

Among the attendees, although I would not know this for years, was a San Francisco poet who hung out with the Auerhahn Press people, Geoffrey Brown, and his girlfriend at the time, Krishna Evans.

He seduced me.

"Each year, I pick a student to be my lover," he said. The small basement apartment in the Haight was dark not because the sun was already setting, but because so little light could get between the buildings of San Francisco. He talked incessantly, at least partly out of nervousness. I hardly knew which story to believe. He claimed to have been illiterate until he was in his teens, later to have become a lawyer. He spoke of being the reincarnation of Jack Spicer, who'd been dead just two years.

Thirty years later, the smell of scotch still repels me.

AFT, local 1352.

The faculty union chapter at San Francisco State in 1981.

Enslavement *is* permitted as punishment for crime.

Rebecca's husband was the sergeant in charge of security at the Federal Correctional Institution in Pleasanton. They lived in a trailer home in a "residential" section of the facility, housing in the area generally costing more than guards could afford. We rarely spoke about what I knew about what their lives might be like. After Rebecca was "riffed" by ComputerLand, Gaylynn would drop off her child at the prison each morning for daycare.

Her husband broke both of her eardrums.

This woman was a co-worker, a nurse at Hospitality House, but it could have been Marti with her out-of-control stalker cop ex-husband, or Mrs. Rodriguez, bleeding to death on her front porch just doors up the street from my own house or any of several other women I've known. Having been raised primarily by women, the ongoing battle between the sexes has always seemed anything but metaphoric.

I used my grant to fix my teeth.

Eating a biscuit in Perkos' cafe on Henderson in Porterville, 1997, I break yet another tooth.

They speak in Farsi at the corner store.

The town of Albany was separated from the Scottish north west corner of Berkeley when the latter was incorporated shortly after the turn of the century because the owners of the Hercules Powder Plant, manufacturers of dynamite, were afraid of the constraints on their business a local governing board might put into place. Later, after the plant had blown up for the last time and the company relocated north of Richmond to a site on which it constructed its own town, Hercules, Ocean Vista, as Albany was briefly known [11] used its geographic linkage and legal separation to create a new community of small, single family homes, most of them constructed in the 1920s.

Many of the early families worked either in the industrial plants that lay close by the bay in Berkeley and Emeryville, dumping raw sewage directly into the waters, or else were the shopkeepers who serviced the people of Berkeley. As the University began to take on an identity as early as the 1930s as a site for such suspect activities as folk music, race mixing and even communism, the natural town-gown distinctions of any college burg were accentuated by the legal divide between the two communities. Albany, by the 1950s, was as much a *not-Berkeley* as it was anything in its own right.

This was reinforced still further by the local clique of Solano and San Pablo Avenue shop owners and realtors who literally governed the place (one of whom was a cousin through marriage to one of my grandfather's nieces). Within walking distance of the University of California campus was a city of 17,000 that was thoroughly red-lined, that housed the northern California headquarters operations for right-wing cabals such as the John Birch Society and the Minutemen. In school, there was a Japanese student in one class, three Hispanics, a Jew and an African American in others, but there proved so few of any single group that each individual was forced to stand for all Others in the school. In Spanish class, our teacher insisted that we speak as she alleged people spoke in Spain and not as they did in Mexico or only a few blocks beyond the border of town, a dialect she no doubt thought of as an Indian mongrelization of a great European tongue.

YPSL.

With the exception of the CP and the larger Trotskyist tendencies, the 1960s rolled over the left formations of the 1950s like a tidal wave over so many sand castles. Unprepared to deal with a popular rebellion to its left and with none of its regard for McCarthy-era caution, an organization like the Young People's Socialist League was rapidly reduced to the alphabet soup of history. Pronounced *YipSL.*

The national question.

The war at home was not an object, but a process, one that reached an apotheosis in the weeks immediately following the murders at Kent and Jackson state universities. At Berkeley, we simply stopped going to classes. At first, everyone stopped going to class. Instead we worked 18-20 hour days organizing canvassing projects throughout the entire East Bay. For a time, we literally stole resources from the buildings—entire printing presses—carrying them to a house north of campus that a handful of English majors shared. After we realized that the "reconstitution" was so total that the regents and school administration simply planned to do nothing in response, no arrests for theft, no lockouts of the now empty buildings, we returned and turned the campus into an antiwar operation the size of the Rouge Plant. Thousands of students participated every day. I ran a silk-screen poster operation out of what had been a classroom in Wheeler Hall, an endless stream of boxy prints that read "Another Home for Peace." The smell of the paint and the curious feeling of participating, being, if not in control, at least active in my own destiny was intoxicating.

Even then, I think I must have realized that I had a penchant for infrastructural projects, as I spent much more time helping groups to go out into the community than I ever did canvassing myself. Once a week, however, I would get out and go door to door, usually in the outer reaches of Contra Costa county. Invariably, I would run across some kid who'd failed to report for induction, but who didn't know that resources existed to contest the draft. We'd stand in the shadows of a porch as he would explain that he was frightened, but that he'd already figured out that whatever the consequences might be, the worst alternative surely was to submit to the draft. I would hand out brochures, explain why I and other students felt it necessary to oppose American intervention in a land that held no strategic value to the United States.

The war itself would continue for another five years, but after the middle of 1970 the question was not one of the outcome, but of the conditions of the American defeat. Although thousands of Americans and millions of Indochinese were still to die, and although the largest marches were still to come, from this point forward everything began to have the air of the foregone conclusion.

Already the left was splintering. As early as 1966, Shelly and I stood in the front yard of our North Oakland cottage and watched the Black Panthers two doors down practicing close order drills, more like a junior high school traffic squad than a military unit. There was, it seemed apparent, no room for us in that world, so how then did our left fit together with it?

Even in the 1960s, one segment of the anti-war movement based their arguments not on the stupidity, cruelty or arrogance of US policy, but on the inherent rights of the Vietnamese, Laotians, Thais and Cambodians, an implicit essentialism of habitation that always made me nervous. The idea that a given people "owned" a particular territory in perpetuity seemed to ignore everything I knew about human migration. The concept even of continental stability seemed only to demonstrate that people could not subjectively experience or recognize geologic time. Within that tendency, there were always some who would portray this or that or another group, first in Indochina, then later in Central and South American, Africa, and the Middle East, in beatific terms. I would run into this same tendency again in an even more virulent form, in the prison movement.

Gradually, I began to realize that with all of the good reasons for political action in the world, even good reasons for supporting the indigenous efforts of local groups in the so-called developing countries, the left would be motivated and even to some degree directed by individuals driven by needs of an entirely different order as well.

I look forward to old age with some excitement.

Sixteen years later, I am writing from room 218 in the Motel Six of Porterville, in the Sierra foothills north of Bakersfield. My nephew, Stephen Matthew Silliman, is just four days old. Allen Ginsberg has been dead for 13 days. Their worlds never crossed, just as mine never crossed Gertrude Stein's. But I know people who have slept with people who have slept with people who slept with Walt Whitman. At 94, Carl

Rakosi's mind clear as a bell. Others at 24, hopelessly muddied and muddled. Once, walking on the beach at Stinson with Rae Armantrout during our student days at Berkeley, I knelt to pick up a beautifully pocked smooth gray stone (I still have it). She asked me what I was doing. "Looking for the good ones," I replied.

42 years for Fibreboard Products.

He was first-line management all the years I was growing up, a foreman in the newspaper pulping operation. Once, sometime in the early '50s, he'd been standing on a four story high stack of papers when the water boom swung and hit him from the rear. He called home to stay he'd be "a little late" for dinner, having broken both wrists and ankles. Later, as his hearing declined, he refused to see a doctor or consider a hearing aid, fearing that they would use this as an excuse to fire him immediately before his retirement. As it happened, he spent the entire last year on the job working to avoid just that result.

Although we drove right past the plant every time we took 80 through Emeryville (there's a tall dark highrise apartment complex there just east of the freeway now), he never took either my brother or I to the job. I never once heard him speak of his work with satisfaction or pleasure.

Food is a weapon.

Nothing in the global marketplace more accurately depicts the pathology of capital than the distribution of survival. This sentence is for Corrine Dufka of Nairobi, Kenya.

Yet the sight of people making love is deeply moving.

Making my rounds of the Tenderloin (which I do, on average, twice a day during the five years I work at Hospitality House), I step into one of the darkest and most rancid of the little porn theaters that crowded around lower Eddy. The room inside is small and for the most part empty. On the screen, 20 feet high, is Kathy Acker. She stands naked against a kitchen counter as a young man, also naked, literally flogs her with a head of iceberg lettuce. She turns, raising herself onto the counter, facing him, so that he can enter her.

Music is essential.

It was a bookish kid's way to discover the world. At 16, a reference in the liner notes to a Kingston Trio album led me to buy a record of someone I'd never heard, or heard of, before—Pete Seeger, which in turn led to Leadbelly, Woody Guthrie, the Weavers, which in turn. . . .

The cops wear shields that serve as masks.

The one time I was injured in the hundreds of demonstrations in which I took part was, in 1970, one of the rare times when I'd decided not to be involved, so was merely milling around the outskirts of an audience of several thousand, listening to the speakers, when the cops rushed the crowd from behind. I didn't even notice them until the baton rapped me across the back, sending me stumbling right through a line of cops. I kept running and got free, but the next morning couldn't get out of bed for the pain. Shelly called John Gorham, who drove me to Herrick Hospital where x-rays suggested a bruised kidney.

Her lungs heavy with asbestos.

Evelyn Schaaf was short, heavy, almost always angry and abrasive. She also had a quick sense of humor and the second loudest laugh in the world. Her husband, Valmar, a civil engineer who financed her political activities and usually served as the president of the board of whatever nonprofit they were running at the time, still liked to identify himself as a "union thug." His laugh is louder. [12]

When, over the phone, I'd first asked her what CPHJ was, she laughed and responded "Two fat ladies!" In fact, there was a core of around a dozen volunteers, most of them older women, all but two widowed or divorced, who'd been galvanized around the death in San Quentin of a young man by the name of Fred Billingslea, an African American who'd suffered a psychotic break in prison—not such an unusual occurrence—and had been screaming in his cell, smearing feces on the wall until the guards came up and fired tear gas canisters into it with shotguns. One canister hit him in the throat and he went down instantly. They moved him unconscious to the prison hospital by dragging him down several flights of stairs by his ankle, his head hitting the concrete and metal steps again and again.

What made CPHJ possible as "alternative military service" was the presence of certain names on the letter head, U.S. Senator John Tunney, plus Congressmen Leo Ryan and Ron Dellums.

My first day on the job, I opened perhaps a hundred letters that had come in the mail from different prisoners, their friends and family, learning the complex code by which these letters were used to document complaints, problems, practices. At the end of the day, I was given a key to the office and told to open it up the next morning and start with the mail as soon as it arrived. But when I got to the office on the second floor of an old legal building on Fourth Street in San Rafael across from the absent original civic center, a nervous man in his mid-forties was literally cowering in the doorway. He was, he said, an escaped prisoner, at least technically. He'd been released to a halfway house at the edge of San Quentin to work for a few months prior to his parole and had obtained work in a local body shop. The boss, thinking he was doing the man a favor, told no one on the staff of the man's situation and one of the administrative workers had invited him home, first for dinner and then to spend the night. After several years away from even the sight of women, the offer proved impossible to decline. But now, with dawn, he realized he'd be reported missing and that the police would be looking for him. "Escape" in those days tended to carry a five-year term.

I opened the office, let him in (I was probably harboring a fugitive), then called Evelyn at home, who suggested a lawyer to call. I did, explaining the situation, and he agreed to phone the prison and arrange a "surrender" if they would agree not to prosecute. They consented and all that remained was to transport the man to the lawyer's office without him getting picked up or arrested in the mean time. So I walked down the hall to the office of Sally Soladay, another lawyer who had been instrumental in the formation of CPHJ (she was the lawyer handling the Billingslea wrongful death action for his family), explaining the circumstances all over again and they agreed that a lawyer should act as his chauffeur. One did. This was my second morning on the job.

Two weeks too old to collect orphan's benefits.

We'd gone into the City to the Haight where Bill said he could score some acid, something I'd been wanting to try for weeks, maybe months. I had no idea what to expect at all—everybody had said the drug was/would be "incredible" but no one had said how exactly, in what fashion. Of the four of us, only Bill had taken it before and he only once. In Chinatown, as the visual elements of the early high began to emerge, my teeth chattering compulsively, I sat cross-legged on Grant Street and watched catfish through the window of a market as they gradually turned into dragons. Every Disney character then in existence was milling around the crowded intersection of Columbus and Grant. We didn't *do* anything—we wandered about, giggly and amazed. Later, after midnight, as the visuals calmed down, we drove back to Berkeley where I decided not to crash on David's couch but instead had Bill drive over to Solano in Albany to the newish apartment complex where my mother now had an apartment.

As I wandered up the stairway, I began to realize that I was still too high to deal with my mom, who might still be awake. Since I stayed at the apartment maybe three or four times per week, it wasn't as though she expected me, or at least this was how I envisioned it. Instead, I took the small door that led up to the roof, looking out over the small town in which I'd grown up, thinking big, vague thoughts. The sense of height and breadth on the rooftop was very close to flying and I recall looking down at the street for a long time, trying to understand why flight had been denied to humans as a species. It seemed so unfair.

At one point, I noticed the television antenna for the complex. I had never realized the sculptural qualities of this wire construction before. It seemed anthropomorphic and very inviting. I sat in front of it and examined it slowly and carefully, and then began methodically to disassemble it, looking at each section of aluminum with a sense of wonder. What *was* aluminum? How could a metal seem so "made" and yet so insubstantial. There was a spiritual quality to the transitory nature of industrial process that I'd never appreciated before. Aluminum clearly was alive—it had an intelligence that took exactly the shape of its being.

For reasons I will never understand, I began singing to myself. I don't recall what, other than that it was a Sinatra tune (although if you'd asked me in 1964 what I thought of Sinatra I would have said that I despised him). I was still humming this as I wandered downstairs and turned the key to the apartment. Inside, the light to the living room was still on, my mother sitting on the couch, looking angrily at me. She accused me of being drunk and reminded me that I wasn't old enough yet to drink. I said nothing since this was a better impression I imagined than telling her the truth. Had she even heard of LSD?

Then she added, almost in the same breath, before I could decide whether or not to trust myself to say anything at all, that she'd gotten a phone call from my uncle in Pasco. My father had been in an accident somewhere in South Carolina. After several days, he'd died. I still didn't say anything, nor did she. I went to the room that was nominally mine and lay on the bed I'd grown up with—the "cottage cheese" stucco and asbestos walls pulsated every shade of the rainbow. I don't recall what I thought—I don't even recall thinking—but I remember looking inside myself, imagining that I should find an emotion somewhere, puzzled a little that I seemed to find none.

This was August 21, 1965. On about this same day in San Francisco (although I would not realize this for years), Jack Spicer died. In Mount Pleasant, South Carolina, it was the tenth birthday of Nancy Silliman.

A woman on the train asks Angela Davis for an autograph.

Some of the passengers on the BART car look up, trying to figure out who the "famous" woman is. I'm sitting half a car away, jotting in a notebook.

You get read your Miranda.

Autobiographer's motto: *You have a right to remain silent.*

As if a correct line would somehow solve the future.

My brother had invited Barbara and I to the Christian commune where he now lived, on the edge of Petaluma. The group was learning how to farm, but at the time (1972) was relatively incompetent at it. City kids, playing country. Barbara, the quintessential suburban princess, had to show someone how to cut off the head of a chicken, which she did quickly, irritated at their lack of understanding of their own actions. Later, during a house meeting, we saw and heard several of the group's members talking in tongues.

Talking with my brother during his early years as a "born again" Christian often felt eerily similar to conversations I had had elsewhere with friends who'd gotten involved with one or another ultraleftist political cult. In each instance, the unassailability of the logic was taken by the speaker as a given, regardless of just how loopy any of the individual statements that followed might be. (The leader of the Sparts, for example, once called the Albanian CP a bunch of "goat fuckers," which gave the Socialist Workers Party—by comparison a "centrist" Trotskyist tendency in those days—occasion to blast the Sparts for ethnic bias, to which the Sparts responded, "well, the Albanians are a peasant people and obviously the SWP doesn't understand peasant life, being just a bunch of petite bourgeois deviationists.")

My brother's sense of my Marxism was never informed by having read much political theory or history. Once, when I was working in the prison movement, he told me that he'd been reading Solzynheitsen's *Gulag Archipelago*. Wasn't communism a repressive system?

Certainly Stalinism was, I replied. For example, look at Castro outlawing homosexuality in Cuba. My brother, who at this stage of his life was still literally leading book-burning demonstrations in front of the Theosophy Book Store in San Francisco, was soon defending Castro. Leucretia, his wife at the time, glowered at me.

They murdered his parents just to make the point.

No week ever went by during my childhood in which my grandmother did not tell me how my father had "ruined" my mother's life.

Long before I ever met Robby or Michael Meeropol, I took the execution of Julius and Ethel Rosenberg as an emblem for cruelty.

It's not easy if your audience doesn't identify as readers.

What I desire in poetry, my own and that of others, is that everyone work as hard as possible, the sort of labor that is indistinguishable from the best play, the most passionate lovemaking, the most intense experience of music or painting or cinema. I am perpetually startled, stunned even, not simply that this desire is not universally shared, but the degree of hostility with which it is so often met.

Mastectomies are done by men.

Cancer has its politics. In the years since I wrote this sentence, I have come to know hundreds of people attacked by the cells of their own bodies. Jerry Estrin never stood a chance.

Our pets live at whim.

I grew up with cats and for years tended to adopt strays, named variously Useless, Topaz, Alto.[13] The cool, dispassionate consideration of an alien species seems to me often the perfect perspective from which to view the human. What I discovered as an adult, however, was that my obsessive self-centeredness didn't translate well to ongoing care of others. Without exception, my cats found neighbors who voluntarily fed them on the back porches and decided that this would become home.

Net income is down 13%.

One's relation to a statistic is invariably both personal and dissociated. At the time I wrote this sentence I was about to leave Hospitality House, where I had worked for five years, to try and live for a year on part-time teaching jobs at San Francisco State and UC San Diego, making ends meet with the money I had saved from my 1979 NEA grant.

Those distant sirens down in the valley signal great hinges in the lives of strangers.

August 18, 1965: three men are working in a small brick building, little more than a room. One of them (my father?) flicks on a switch when he shouldn't. 23,000 volts flail through the air setting off an explosion so intense that the piping on the wall melts. My father gets up and staggers outside, eventually into an ambulance, third degree burns over eighty percent of his body. It's the toxins in his blood from all the burned tissue that kills him three days later, kidney failure. "He kissed me good-bye, went to work and never came home," says Buddy, the half brother I won't meet even by telephone for another 31 years.

A phone tree.

The ability to differentiate and to organize that differentiation is the essence of politics as a practice. We'd borrow the law offices of friends, bring in some pizzas and Cokes, and hit the phones from 6 until 9, night after night. The list in front of us might include every "high probability voter" registered as a Democrat in a multi-unit building (and therefore a renter) in a middle- or lower-income neighborhood. (In the "better" neighborhoods, we'd run into tenants who identified as *future* owners and who were therefore much less apt to vote for their own immediate self-interest.)

The landlord's control of terror is implicit.

As a member of the Arson Task Force of the San Francisco Fire Department, I helped to construct a list of landlords whose "problem" tenants always seemed to have fires, so that henceforward any fire in one of their buildings would automatically initiate an arson investigation. My own landlord showed up on the list.

Not just a party but a culture.

A quotation of Jim Shoch (citing perhaps Stanley Aronowitz) on why the American Communist Party had a lasting impact where other radical organizations did not (especially notable when one considers the deformed nature of the revolution that the CP was forced to support). This principle is also why an internationalist poetry of urban centers—the essence of the avant-garde tradition—holds such a strong attraction for me.

Copayment.

Telephone message, Friday, June 6, 1997: "Hello. You may not know me, but my name is Ron Silliman. If you are the Glenn

Silliman who is the son of Glenn Sherman Silliman, born in Prosser, Washington, and who died in Mount Pleasant in August of 1965, then I am your older brother." Within an hour, Buddy's sister (I did not know for certain that she was his full sister, that he even knew her, that she was still alive, even what her last name might be), *my* sister, calls Krishna at my home number, saying, "Hello. My name is Nancy Silliman Bryant and I am not a crackpot."

He held the Magnum with both hands and ordered me to stop.

I did and immediately he spread-eagled me against a pastel sedan parked at the curb, crooking his neck just slightly to talk into a speaker mounted on his epaulet: "Got him."

This soon produced two men in their early thirties who looked as if they had just come from a golf course. They identified themselves as members of the FBI and asked me where I had stashed the gun and the money. I stammered my reply in the form of a question—*what gun, what money?* From the bank, one of them replied, nodding back toward Solano, the commercial strip a block north. There was a Wells Fargo at the end of the block.

By now a police car had arrived and those neighbors of mine who were already home from work began milling on their porches. We'd only been living in the house across the street for a few weeks and had been anxious, as the first student household in a notably middle-class neighborhood, to make a good impression. I'd been on my way to meet Shelly and her friend Brandi for dinner and had thought to bring a joint with me as a gift for the meal. Now I was relieved that

I'd decided against it. I denied everything and they told me not to be a smart ass.

The original officer who stopped me, a light-skinned African American somewhat smaller than myself, was on his radio again, trying to convince a bank officer to walk a single block to make the positive i.d. before they took me downtown. Apparently the manager was reluctant because the officer was explaining that he understood that it was after hours and that the day had been harrowing enough with the robbery. The FBI twins were pawing through my wallet. I was sweating and shaking like a leaf, but I wasn't handcuffed or spread-eagled any more. I explained who I was and where I lived and what I was doing and asked why they thought I would be dumb enough to rob the bank on my own block. Because you go to UC, the second agent sneered.

Finally an older man in a cheap dark suit arrived, the branch manager. "Yes I said the robber had long blond hair," he sneered, visibly upset, "but I also said it was a woman." Even after he left, they kept me on the corner for another twenty minutes while they checked to see if I had any outstanding problems with the draft.

The garden is a luxury (a civilization of snail and spider).

At dawn or maybe even a little before, I sit on a chair out on the porch, watching woodpeckers hop up and down the bark of the black oak, the trees beginning to fill with the songs of birds. A hawk's silhouette is visible on a branch further down the hill. In the distance behind me, barely audible, is the clickety rattle of a train heading to Harrisburg.

They call their clubs batons.

Prior to swarming onto campus, the cops and deputy sheriffs would cluster around behind the administration building, swinging their clubs idly, like baseball players preparing to bat. The element of sport was visible in the air.

They call their committees clubs.

The Communist Party by the 1970s was a pathetic thing, at its core a collection of seniors with relatively little capacity left for direct political organizing, still ignoring the crimes of Stalinism and deeply committed to a politics of duplicity. Around these old Lincoln Brigade vets were a younger circle of African American activists—Angela Davis is the name everyone recognizes—actually attempting to use the resources of this ancient organization. Characteristically, every left movement in the Bay Area had one or two CP members whose job it was to be supportive of the movement and report back to the organization on our "progress" in on-the-ground socialism. There was always a limit to how much we would trust the obvious CP member, who would never, of course, admit that this was his or her role. Their behavior was very much like that of police infiltrators but without the crazed provocatism. From some of them, I gradually got an image of what a lifetime committed to the left might look like.

Her friendships with women are different.

I've come to appreciate this even more over time. When we moved to Pennsylvania in 1995, I had my job as ready social net into which I could fit. Being a poet also provides one with a sense of a community in many different cities. In addition to Bob and Francie, who we knew from Berkeley, and Howie who'd been on the *Socialist Review* editorial collective and his wife Debbie, who'd worked at Hospitality House, there were Gil and Julia and Rachel and Eli. I also used email a lot, and could walk to the Paoli Amtrak station and find myself in midtown Manhattan with no difficulty.

In the 20 years I've known Krishna she's made only two new close friendships. To be physically removed from most of them is a serious dislocation in a way that is completely unlike anything I've ever experienced.

Talking so much is oppressive.

I get loud when I get anxious. Later I wish I hadn't.

Outplacement.

Everyone has figured out a theory by which they won't be the individual laid off, even as they understand that cuts are coming and that this round will be steep. After they learn, a few go around saying good-bye to the survivors while others clear their desks out almost instantly, as if shamed. Tauscher, the bulky CEO of Vanstar, loved to use the phrase "by the end of the day" to punctuate his speeches, even after it got to be a joke with the staffers who had seen over 50 vice-presidents "churn" over less than seven years. "By the end of the day, we'll all be riffed," said Kit, making a verb of the acronym for Reduction in Force. And eventually he was.

A shadowy locked facility using drugs and double-celling (a rest home).

The woman in the next room moaned endlessly, unconscious even of her moaning. My grandmother, who had known her for decades, seldom even referred to her now. Her eyes darted around the room even as they failed to see all but a few peripheral shadows and bursts of light. On the far side of her own room sat her older sister, who from time to time would burst out with a question—"who is that?"—which my grandmother would answer only by scolding her, "Oh, you know who this is!" or "I've already told you a dozen times!" I would sit quietly. On a few occasions, I would read to her from a book about a cat detective.

That was the Sunday Henry's father murdered his wife on the front porch.

For this he received six months in prison and was soon back at the same factory as my grandfather, where he worked as a janitor. The explanation was that the boys were not his children and for her to threaten to walk out and to leave them behind had been unthinkable. Patiently, my brother tried to teach Henry to read, using adventure comic books. Later, Henry and his brother sodomized the boy next door to us with a wooden board. The last I heard of him, a year or two after high school, the Hell's Angels were looking for him: he'd knocked a member's eye out with a hammer.

If it demonstrates form they can't read it.

The reception of my writing can be divided easily into two periods—before the publication of *Ketjak* in 1978 and after. I'd been toying with the idea of a larger prose poem and the idea of something programmatic. I wanted to attack what I saw as the *sweetness* of Stein and Mac Low's dependency upon restricted vocabularies (as in, say, an insurance tract—*Stanzas for Iris Lezak* was still a new publication in 1974). The problem was how to begin.

One evening, Barry and I went to the Asian Art Museum in Golden Gate Park to hear a concert in its auditorium, the west coast debut of Steve Reich's *Drumming*. It was the third Reich performance I'd attended, the others being Paul Zukofsky's performance of *Violin Phase* on my 21st birthday on the UC campus (several listeners walked out, led by, of all people, Mario Savio) and a "tape performance" of several loops (including *Come Out*, the work of his I'd first discovered on a record) at the newly opened University Art Museum in Berkeley.

As *Drumming* began and proceeded (augmented by the room's almost perfect acoustics), I began to sense, for the first time, exactly what the formal structure of *Ketjak* would be. Within a week I was beginning to scribble out ideas and, finally, on my way to meet my ex-wife Shelly (we were to meet on the steps of the Bank of America headquarters), I began to write in a cheap notebook, my first sentence inspired by the B of A's architecture, "Revolving door."

If it demonstrates mercy they have something worse in mind.

Unquestionably, the key word in *Albany* is "if." Every one of the sentences around which the work is organized begins with this word.

Twice, carelessness has led to abortion.

She's talking to me on the telephone from Ashville, explaining matter of factly that she's heading tomorrow for Atlanta, where the procedure can be performed legally and safely, her voice drained of any emotion, and I realize, three thousand miles to the west, that we will never be a couple again, that it has never even occurred to her to ask me what I think.

To own a basement.

After high school, I would pile into a car with some friends at least once or twice a week and we'd cruise up into the Berkeley hills to look at the houses that we declared we would own once we grew up. These homes ranged from the utterly middle class to faux mansions, many of them in 1920s Craftsman style, in contrast with which the small thousand-square-foot house I shared with four members of three separate generations felt like a shoebox. Or worse. The idea of a basement when I wrote this sentence maybe twelve years later was that of a completely inessential element of housing. Since so many of the people I knew at that point in San Francisco were crammed into shared living arrangements, the idea of owning something that could include the inessential seemed unfathomable.

I am writing at this moment in the finished basement of a split level house with 2600 square feet (not counting a two-car garage) on a half acre of land in the outer Philadelphia suburbs.

Nor is the sky any less constructed.

As simple as the recognition that neither the sun nor moon ever really "rises" or "sets." The idea of "constellations." How quickly we forget how the city lights erase so many stars even on the clearest of nights.

The design of a department store is intended to leave you fragmented, off-balance.

David Antin has compared this to the new sentence. But retail design is an art. A department store is an elaborately spatialized narrative—the last sentence is always the same: *you buy.*

A lit drop.

On Saturday mornings throughout the late 1970s, I would spend three or four hours with between 20 and 50 like-minded souls walking San Francisco precincts for the New American Movement. More often than not, the operation was contributed to another group: a labor union, a political candidate, the coalition supporting or opposing some measure on the ballot. With San Francisco's local elections in odd years and California's general tendency toward propositions at all levels, there was literally always something to be contested. Rent control, district election of county supervisors and homophobic (or otherwise reactionary) state measures seemed constant.

The New American Movement (NAM) had been started earlier in the seventies by former members of SDS. Having for the most part dropped out of school to take activist jobs in the cities, they found themselves first without the grounding orientation of campus life itself and then without the more immediate context that an organization like SDS had provided.

But SDS had never played a significant role in the Bay Area, largely because the 1960s left had grown up around the anti-HUAC[14] demonstrations of 1960, the CORE integration actions of the early sixties, the Free Speech Movement at Berkeley in 1964 and the first Vietnam Day Teach-In a year later. With no particular need for SDS to serve as a catalyst for political revolt—the role it played in so many other cities and campuses—the organization had little real focus in the Bay Area and became instead a front for the local branch of the pseudo-Maoist Progressive Labor Party.

Still, by the early 1970s, the diaspora of campus politicos had taken effect in the Bay Area as well. While the prison movement was somewhat unusual in that its activists tended not to have come from the campuses, but rather tended to be homegrown (*organic*, in Gramsci's terms), the tenants movement and others were filled with former students who both wanted a means of looking at their own daily work critically while connecting up the many small left-leaning organizations into something we all still fantasized as a mass phenomenon.

While working in the prison movement, I'd attended some of the local pre-formation meetings of NAM, but was still wary of any organizations with a specific ideological line as I'd always felt such groups, almost irregardless of what the line might have been, to be manipulative in their use of people and issues almost invariably counterproductive to the building of a larger left coalition. The presence of people I'd long since learned to distrust at Berkeley, such as Michael Lerner, put me off even further. Working 60 and 70 hours weeks, plus the long bus rides either to San Rafael or Sacramento from the City on a daily basis made it easy just to ignore the idea.

But after I'd taken a year off and then gone to work at Hospitality House in the Tenderloin, at first with an ostensibly nonpolitical job working on a neighborhood ethnography, I'd begun to wonder what the connection between my job, the obvious social needs of the people in whose neighborhood I spent eight to ten hours every day, my writing, and a larger sense of meaning, I began to look around for something that could tie these diverse aspects of my self back together. Several of the young lawyers who were active in the housing movement (conversion of residential hotels into tourist use was a burning issue in 1978) were members of NAM as was the newly hired political organizer for the local chapter of the Gray Panthers, Jim Shoch.

Shoch was someone I'd heard about over the years. He'd been tossed out of Stanford for his involvement in Bruce Franklin's Venceremos Brigade, the same group (yet another variation on Maoism) that had adopted Popeye Jackson's United Prisoners Union. Later I'd see his name in connection with a left-wing newspaper in San Francisco that had more or less plagiarized some of my writing on prisons verbatim. Since the purpose of those pieces was to create direct political pressure, I'd not been offended.

The potential of placing as many as 50 volunteers for a lit drop week in and week out put NAM almost on a par with any labor union in the City as far as most liberal politicians were concerned. A significant portion of the local pols would join just before election, as they did the various gay, Asian, African American and Latino Democratic Clubs. Others, including Barbara Boxer, were happy to have the support on the weekends, but made it manifestly clear that they never wanted NAM's endorsement or to be associated formally with something that looked like a socialist organization.

On Saturdays we'd walk precincts, starting off with a forty-five minute or so milling around and orientation over coffee and donuts. Then, in pairs, we'd pick a precinct and get whatever the week's flyers or brochures were and head out, sometimes by car, often by bus. On a couple of Sunday evenings each month, NAM would have a chapter meeting, where as many as sixty members would gather, usually at the Socialist School offices in the Mission, to debate topics, discuss a possible merger with Michael Harrington's Democratic Socialist Organizing Committee (DSOC), and occasionally to endorse candidates or propositions for a forthcoming ballot. It was an easy schedule for a single person to fall into, although it was a curiously male world.[15]

One day sometime around 1978, Walter Park, a DSOC activist and single parent, got himself a small computer kit (probably a Heath Kit). As primitive as this pre-DOS machine was, it enabled Park to develop specialized mailing lists without having to type names over and over on photocopying labels. Households with Spanish surnames, households in which all registered voters were male (or female), households in multi-unit buildings.

Within 18 months, Park was the county chair of the Jimmy Carter re-election campaign (San Francisco being one of the few districts Carter would carry in that election) and the frequency of lit drops began to decline, replaced by direct mail and the phone bank.

I left Hospitality House in 1981 in order to teach for year (first at San Francisco State, later at UC San Diego). When I came back, I spent about four months looking for new job and began to work again with the newly merged Democratic Socialists of America that now combined NAM and DSOC. When Shoch or perhaps Mitch Omerberg announced that they needed a volunteer to handle the mailing list and that the list was on Park's computer in the offices of the Independent Housing Service (a group that located, tracked and otherwise promoted wheelchair accessible apartments) in the Tenderloin, but could only be used after hours, I volunteered on the spot. Computers, I had decided, were something that I needed to understand. I had already seen them transform the structure of left political activity in San Francisco. At the time, the IBM PC and the Apple Macintosh were each less than two years old.

They photograph Habermas to hide the hairlip.

We *improve* our heroes out of no need of their own. This is why, at least in part, the reaction to any statement that seems to attack this defended image is met with such fierce opposition.

The verb *to be* admits the assertion.

"Use active language" is precisely kind of bad advice creative writing programs still shovel out with no shame and even less contemplation. That single verb form that invokes the passive tense acknowledges the presence of a writing mind.

It was Grenier's intransigence, his absolute horror at the conventionally literary that made me realize that I would not become a serious or mature writer in any fashion until I was ready to embrace everything I had ever been warned against.

The body is a prison, a garden.

Should you someday die of a "natural" cause, then that which will kill you is present already within your system.

Once each year I pass, without celebrating, the anniversary of my death.

In kind.

In 1972, I lived on less than $150 per month, the following year barely any more.[16] My third year out of college and in the prison movement saw my wages nearly double—to $250 per month. By the time I left CPHJ in 1977, I was earning all of $450, more than some of the lawyers in the political collectives around town, but barely anything to live on as San Francisco rents skyrocketed.

This only deepened the irrational feelings (the inability of the starving person to ever feel full at a banquet) I carried with me from my childhood. I felt exploited and angry because my comrades at CPHJ, most of whom (and all those in positions of power) either had independent sources of income themselves or were married to men who paid all the bills while they carried on the "good fight" as volunteers, never moved to raise a single cent unless and until the organization was on the brink of collapse for want of it. I was, with less than a dozen other people, rewriting the entire sentencing section of the California penal code, worrying every day about the consequences of the slightest rewording of a paragraph on hundreds of lives, men and women and their families who would all have to live with the consequences of our work. But often at the end of a long day in Sacramento, walking back to the Greyhound Station for the two-hour ride to San Francisco, I found myself barely able to get a taco in a fast food joint.

I get back to the City too late to go to a reading, too poor to buy a new book and often feeling totally disconnected from my roommates, none of whom (with the two notable exceptions of Elliot Helfer and Barrett Watten) ever seemed to realize the psychic weight I carried around with me.

At Hospitality House, the dynamics had been fairly similar. The board was willing to work to raise enough funding to pay the staff whatever the minimum was that would keep them coming back to keep the agency running. Barely making the minimum wage, these were the hardest working and smartest co-workers I would ever have. In five years at HH, as the staff always called it, I worked on a small coalition that saved over 10,000 units of low-income housing.

After I left Hospitality House to teach for a year, I made a decision that whatever job I returned to in the non-profit world would have a significant fundraising element. I was no longer going to leave it to others to determine whether or not I had enough money to go the dentist or a movie or eat fish. This was how I ended up as the director of development for a graduate school focusing on East-West religions, the California Institute of Integral Studies, and how I came to meet Hank Rosso, the man who professionalized nonprofit fundraising in America and who, in his own quiet way, taught me almost everything I would ever know about marketing.

Client populations (cross the tundra).

Once known as Saint Anne's Valley, a residential district in which Robert Frost, Isadora Duncan and Alice B. Toklas had been born, the presence of brothels had given the Tenderloin its name by the 1890s. In the 1930s, the TL was the first gay neighborhood, as such, in the United States. In the 1950s and '60s, as the merchant marine district South of Market[17] was plowed under and increasingly fewer men were able to get jobs at sea, the TL became an overflow receptacle for these mostly alcoholic drifters just a few blocks north of their old homes. Also in the 1950s, senior citizens began to arrive, unwilling to move about with their children as the post-war economic boom all but erased the three- and four-generation household. Later in the '60s, as the Haight filled beyond capacity with suburban youth and a brief 1966 riot at the corner of Divisadero and McAllister led San Francisco to "redevelop" the Fillmore district as they had SOMA, African Americans and the more isolated hippies began to fill the community. In the 1970s, as Ronald Reagan and Jerry Brown emptied the state's mental hospitals[18], the neighborhood changed again. By the end of the decade, Indochinese refugees began to slowly fill the residential hotels and apartment buildings. A family of nine, each receiving funds from the Indochinese Resettlement Assistance Program, could pay considerably more for a one-bedroom apartment than the single psychotic. But if the social ecology of the neighborhood was fragile, some portion of each group lingered on until the human texture of these 44 city blocks and 19,000 people became as rich a soil as I have ever seen. Before a new hotel went in kitty-corner from the 5th and Market Bart station, there was a tavern that catered exclusively to transvestites and transsexuals of color, and the men who loved them. The corner of Leavenworth and Eddy was devoted almost exclusively to the pursuit of heroin. Street walkers generally worked east of Leavenworth because the far side of that street marked the boundary of the Northern Precinct, whose cops had a bad reputation for "bruising the merchandise." The mob ran a couple of bars and eateries by the hotels, but was more visible around the porn shops and massage parlors. The homeless began to multiply toward the end of the Carter regime.

These people were my friends: *John Rhodes*, a deeply hallucinatory young man, in his better moments a fine potter in Krishna's arts program, who, having been denied SSI for months, finally got his back payments all at once and went and purchased a used car, only to kill someone in an accident within hours, imagining that a herd of white horses was racing toward him down the street. *Bob Grove*, a onetime social worker on parole for manslaughter who once forced me to invent the "no gun in class" rule for the Tenderloin Writers Workshop (later, as he was walking near Polk Street wearing a cowboy hat one night, three kids from Contra Costa County, in town to harass gays, mistook him as an easy mark and began to play catch with Bob's hat until he pulled out his pistol and shot them, leaving one paralyzed from the waist down). *Sunbeam*, who changed her name to Rainbow whenever she was on Prolixin. *Spider*, whose real name was James Taylor though people only called him that to tease him, who could scrawl 20 pages of densely visual run-on sentences in his hotel room each night, mounting great comic-book style car crash novels, not one of which I was ever able to get him to type up. *Harley Kohler*, a tiny crossdressing writer of sonnets, a sort of lumpen language poet avant le lettre, whose lover Keith (long dead of AIDS) had once been an attendant in the first group home Larry Eigner stayed in upon his arrival in Berkeley. *Sandy*, a heavy young woman just marginally able to get by on a daily basis, who picked up a boyfriend who wanted to ride freight trains with her to the Mardi Gras. When I next saw her, one hand was missing, severed under the wheels of a locomotive. *Frieda Biery*, a German woman who'd married a farmer from upstate New York and lived with him until well into her late sixties before deciding to hell with his drinking and abuse, riding west in a VW minibus with her son. She would attend the Writers Workshop and knit quietly, saying little. Her small dog, her mode of protection, would sleep at her feet. After a story finished, she would make a comment as if in passing, to the effect of "I think all junkies should be locked up—present company excepted—don't you?" *Gary Mason*, in his thirties, perpetually struggling to stay with his methadone program (once, when I was living in the Mission and had been after my landlord for years to paint our building, I opened the window one morning to discover the scaffolding going up, Gary doing the work). *Anna Krivonic*, a minuscule older woman with a deep, scratchy baritone voice, who wrote doggerel, not quite with the panache of a Helen Adam. Anna lived in one of the local senior hotels and was a regular at almost every writers workshop in the City. After her son died of AIDS, I seldom saw her sober. *Janice*, one of the displaced mentally ill. During the Carter years, she could afford a hotel room on her SSI payments, but often was 86'd after getting into some screaming match with another tenant. By the early 1980s, she'd become a true bag lady. I'd see her on the street and she wouldn't recognize me. *Stephen Brady*, a child whose mother was herself just getting by, obtaining and losing jobs almost monthly, living in small hotels. (Steve's sister died in a fire in one such hotel.) Twelve or thereabouts when I first met him, Steve became independent early as his mother also gradually descended into living with a shopping cart in the street. In order to get away from the gangs in his high school, Brady tested out at 16, got a job in one of the neighborhood hotels and worked in the hotel industry into his thirties, putting himself slowly through San Francisco State and then Berkeley. I see an enormous amount of myself whenever I look at him. *Ray Vingieux*, the secretary for several years for the North of Market Planning Coalition, who'd done twelve years and a day for shooting a cop in a robbery and felt an enormous sense of injustice given that the average term for murder one in those days was itself twelve years and the cop had returned to his beat within weeks. *Mary Tallmountain*, an Eskimo woman with an enormous sense of grace and decorum. She tended to spend half of the year in a local senior hotel, then the rest of it traveling, sometimes back to her native Alaska. While editing the *Tenderloin Times*, I ran a novel based on life in hotel in serial format. Many of her poems were anthologized in collections of Native American writing toward the end of her life. *Phil Evans*, a retired printer who lived in the same hotel as Anna Krivonic (each thought the other was nuts). Phil had worked printing one of the daily papers in Chicago all his life, then retired to San Francisco. After he died on Christmas Day, 1978, someone found an enormous number of perfume bottles in his room. He'd apparently been drinking them. *Al Gellart*, a tiny, cranky little man who liked to show people his photographs of the last lynching in the Bay Area, in San Jose in the 1930s. It was never clear if Al had been part of the mob, but it seemed likely. He lived in several different hotels, but, once, after finding his room in one whose walls were literally pulsing with a solid surface of cockroaches, Dorothy and Krishna and I pushed and finally got him to move into one of the agency-run senior facilities.

Off the books.

The idea of poetry as a "career" in a society that doesn't value literacy is an inherent contradiction. I have worked as an encyclopedia salesman (I quit after two weeks, having sold none, after a lawyer I knew showed me how the pitch I was trained to give "mooches" was a modest form of fraud), a shipping clerk, an accounting clerk, a mail sorter, an amanuensis for blind graduate students, a janitor for Giant Hamburgers (I wouldn't eat hamburgers for years after), a reader for a junior college anthropology course, a case worker and then lobbyist for the prison movement, an editor, production person, occasional writer and even astrologer for an early gay bar paper ("Now is the weather for leather"), a newspaper editor, housing activist, writing teacher, director of development and college administrator, editor of the *Socialist Review* and finally marketeer and analyst in the computer services industry.

The whole neighborhood is empty in the daytime.

At the time I wrote this, I understood this sentence as a comment on the social uses of urban space. With hindsight, I see it now also as a remark on class. The suburbs are full in the middle of the day in ways that an urban working class neighborhood like Bernal Heights in San Francisco is not.

Children form lines at the end of each recess.

Many of my memories of elementary school in the 1950s are tinged with a sense of the implicit *militarism* of daily life.

The junior crossing guard squad of which I was so briefly a member spent half of its time mimicking military drill teams.[19] The scouts, which I shunned at every level, seemed to me a paramilitary organization. Even Little League seemed to me totalitarian (although, ultimately, what kept me from it was the sense I always had around games of angry fathers directing everything—the idea of a father of any sort, especially furious and browbeating, totally intimidated me).

Eminent domain.

After the episode in which my grandmother came after me with a knife, I left for New York and my mother and brother finally did what should have been done a decade earlier— moved to an apartment of their own. It was an incredibly small and dark place that was literally the rear of a mom-and-pop store a block from the El Cerrito Plaza and had already been marked for demolition in order for the Bart tracks to go up. Living there, however fitfully, after I got back from the East was the strangest experience. The family that owned the little store had already moved and were permitting their stock gradually to run down, restocking a little less each week. In some sense, the store had already become a kind of ghost. Immediately out back were the Santa Fe tracks and, once I learned how slowly the trains moved past the Plaza, I started hopping them for the two-mile ride to University Avenue.

Rotating chair.

I receive a photocopy of a letter today, angry, accusative, directed not at me but at Charles Bernstein for having somehow traded on a friendship with Robert Creeley to obtain a job at SUNY Buffalo. Inside the envelope is the fragment of another envelope addressed to Professor Ron Silliman, Dept. of English, University of Pennsylvania, over which in pencil has been written "Unknown/Not at this address." On the flip side of this scrap of envelope is typed "If not at UPenn, what are you doing living at the end of the 'Main Line'?"

Something like this happens two or three times each year—absolute paranoia combined with a sense of outrage, entirely innocent of the facts. The author of this screed has actually published well over a dozen books, several with major trade and university presses, but he is convinced that I (and no doubt others, many others) have obtained something that he cannot and that this must have been done through some underhanded, conspiratorial fashion.

The history of Poland in 90 seconds.

My brother and I would sit in the rear of the Pontiac as my grandfather drove around, doing chores. He very seldom would talk to us, listening instead to one of the AM radio stations that focused on news. (FM was still an oddity that we didn't have until 1958.) As the days wore on, I grew used to the rhythm of hearing minimalist updates of this or that story. I recall being riveted by the contest between Estes Kefauver and Hubert Humphrey at the 1956 Democratic Convention, at the death of Pope Pius XII and the selection of his successor, at the arrival of Castro victorious in Havana (reported at first with some sympathy since he was thought of then as a "reformer" and not a "Marxist"—even the *Readers Digest* ran a friendly interview). I was in the gradual process of becoming not only a news junky, as I remain to this day, but also of listening to the rhythms of a particular narrative style.

Flaming pintos.

A sentence without apparent context is difficult to place, difficult to weigh. A sentence without a verb even more so. In the context of the poem, this fragment seems to be about the lethal nature of corporate irresponsibility, about the automobile as an icon, and the possibility of some sort of ironic twist in the trivialization that occurs by making the phenomenon plural. What motivated the sentence was a discussion I had at a party with Mark Dowie, the journalist who first reported the Pinto's problem with exploding gas tanks. The scion of a liquor fortune with Robert Redford-rugged blond good looks, Mark had been the very timid and tentative compiler of a pamphlet on community resources for ex-prisoners and I had given him some advice on the project. His presentation of self changed dramatically after his research into the depredations of Ford received national attention, rending him the opportunity to bring his upbringing to bear in the new role of Expert. Soon, though, it became apparent that instead of being characterized as a new heavyweight journalist, he would be known instead as the "guy who broke the Pinto story," regardless of how much good effort he put into anything else. This sentence is, in fact, what Mark told me would eventually be engraved on his tombstone.

There is no such place as the economy, the self.

If a lion could speak, it would talk very slowly. Civilization constructed of complex nouns for which no exact equivalent in nature can be found. Identity is composed of our response, passionate or amibivalent, to exactly such muddy notions. Reading *Poetry Flash* with the photograph of Barrett looking boyish and introspective, I remember someone (Kit? Alan? Steve?) saying aloud "It looks like we've been named."

That bird demonstrates the sky.

One way to view nature that incorporates both chance and change. Define the trail by that which is transient. Also, it's something Krishna and I both enjoy and at which neither (for once) is an expert. What is better than a northern flicker at the suet cake? The Virginia rail, perfectly still in the muddy reeds. The long parsed tail of the tropic bird. Once in a bed-and-breakfast, exhausted after a long day of seeking the worm eating warbler in a vacant lot in Davenport, Krishna had an ectopic pregnancy, the fallopian tube literally exploding, and nearly died.

Our home, we were told, had been broken, but who were these people we lived with?

My grandparents had no idea that they would ever be asked to raise a second family and my grandfather's lapsed Catholicism turned his own guilt into open disapproval at my mother's failed marriage. Also, he'd never raised boys and as the youngest in his own family, did not understand how one might nurture anyone younger. Eleven hundred square feet and two bedrooms did not divide easily into five people and three generations. As his hearing declined, he became quieter and quieter, a simmering, seething presence that never quite managed to erupt. My last two years of high school, I probably said less than 100 words to the man. Six weeks after graduation, I was gone.

Clubbed in the stomach, she miscarried.

The whim of existence: my grandmother was the youngest of 13. Two years later, her father was dead. My parents would never have met without the geographic and social dislocations created by the Second World War. They almost certainly would not have married without the mutually damaged home situations each was escaping. My brother and I were each the result of failed birth control. Had my father remained at home, it is unlikely that I ever would have gone to college. Had my father remained at home, I would have learned to love camping and become good with weapons. If I had not grown up on the fringes of Berkeley, it is unlikely that I would have ever stumbled across William Carlos Williams (most Americans never do). Had it not been Berkeley, Shelly would never have arrived in search of a student movement. Had I not turned on the television, would I ever had discovered Zukofsky? Had I not been in New York on the literal day of the Gulf of Tonkin incident, would I have thought to have gotten a draft counselor early enough to have made a difference? Had I not been reading to the blind, would I have stopped in the classroom doorway at Boalt to listen to Fay Stender talking about the San Quentin Six case and would I, six months later, have thought to have sought my conscientious objector's slot with a prison movement group? Had I not had to take the bus to Sacramento so many early mornings, would I have ever walked past Hospitality House and stared in at its windows filled with street people artwork and thought, years after, to have sought a CETA job there? What if I had not stopped drinking? *What if Jon Arnold had not invented metalanguage in front of me, a ten year old boy, as though on his own?*

I wrote this sentence thinking of David Mandel's sister-in-law, beaten at the Oakland Induction Center. Today I read the same sentence inside out.

There were bayonets on campus, cows in India, people shoplifting books.

One night, as the cops were approaching slowly in a vehicle that somehow spewed pepper fog, a particularly acrid and painful form of tear gas, as I was rushing with others to drag some saw horses from a nearby construction sight to create a blockade on Bancroft, I looked up to see that the person who was lifting the other end of the wooden beast was a fellow I'd known as a bully in highschool (he'd once, in a fit of anger—I'd let a teacher who was a friend know that some students had obtained a copy of a forthcoming test—shoved me literally down a flight of stairs). Our eyes locked briefly and the air seemed full of the sounds of sirens, breaking glass, shouting people, rocks bouncing of all manner of surfaces and, more distant, the bullhorn of the first prowl car intoning that "this is an illegal assembly." We stared just long enough to realize what we were doing and who we were, then we rushed with the sawhorse (its yellow blinker flashing all the while) and hurled it atop the mounting pile of other debris. As the car approached, we could begin to smell the fog and dashed with the rest of the crowd back down the side street to the next instant of engagement. I never saw him again.

I just want to make it to lunch time.

A typical day at the office: I arrive a few minutes after the designated hour of eight, plug in my ThinkPad, unlock one or two of the eleven filing cabinets I use on a daily basis, and log on to one of two email systems. The first, a mainframe system called PROFS, also connects me to internal postings from a wide range of other IBM divisions and subsidiaries. If one or two postings from the hundred or so I will scan seems pertinent to our division, I will download it. After PROFS and Lotus Notes, I log onto the internet and scan headlines from a variety of news sources, including the *New York Times*, *Washington Post*, BusinessWire, Reuters and several computing journals (with special attention to *Computer Reseller News* and *Information Week*). By 10:00 or 10:30, I will have scanned between 500 and 700 articles, maybe taking note of six or eight. On some days at this point, I will begin (or continue) to work on a periodic email publication I write. On others, I will turn to research one of the inquiries I've received from other departments, executives, sales reps and managers in the field. An inquiry can take anywhere between five minutes and two weeks to complete. As details emerge during the day from these sources, I may update a series of ongoing presentation files.[20] Most often I use lunch to look at my hard copy mail—computer magazines, research reports, direct mail for events, the occasional invoice. The further each day proceeds, the more apt I am to be pulled into meetings, to conduct consultations for various departments, to embark on "out of the ordinary" projects. At least one hour over the day is given to talking to reps, managers and industry analysts about various "issues." There are always between six and ten of these in an ongoing state at any given moment. By 4:00, I begin to sense whether one or another will lend itself to a concentrated effort in the early evening, once the secretaries and hourly workers depart around 5:30. If so, I plot it out and work until 7:00.

Uncritical of nationalist movements in the Third World.

The world is a system, complete.[21] In spite of Marx's comments about the impossibility of socialism in one country, the left has repeatedly rallied around attempts to set up just such a logical contradiction. Invariably these attempts fail—capital demonstrates its power to undermine any local effort, regardless of how well intentioned it might be. During the Cold War, the U.S. posture of isolating and threatening pockets of resistance, particularly those within what it imagined grandiosely to be have been its own sphere of influence, Asia and the Pacific, forced the smaller power to over-militarize. The most militaristic and least democratic groups within that nation were thus rewarded, promoted, reinforced.[22] The impact on the civilian populace was (also invariably) predictable. Instead of critiquing these deformations and supporting what were now dissident forces within these tiny countries, the U.S. left, stuck on a simplistic the-enemy-of-my-enemy kind of thinking, tended to excuse the excesses (the North Vietnamese hunt down and execute Trotskyists), even to imitate them at home.

Letting the dishes sit for a week.

I was raised in a world in which the dinner was always on time and always predicted: on Friday there would be fish sticks. Even now, over 30 years after leaving home, I am torn —always—by the desire for intense order and its exact opposite.

Macho culture of convicts.

Because her former husband, a San Francisco beat cop, had on more than one occasion tailed her off-duty and at least once come to her job to ask her supervisor if they knew that she was involved with "revolutionaries," Marti's gone to court to get a restraining order. The irony was that her fling with Wilbur "Popeye" Jackson, the head of the nominally Maoist United Prisoners Union (UPU), had been short lived. What lasted was her distrust of the police, which Jackson shared but hardly had created.

The UPU had splintered off from the larger Prisoners Union in 1970 after a meeting to which, it was rumored, both sides brought guns. The Prisoners Union's goals were clear, defined and in retrospect relatively modest. It did not seek an end to prisons, nor critique the social concept of incarceration, but wanted to define and defend the civil rights of prisoners both in the joint and afterward. Focusing on eliminating the byzantine vagaries of the indeterminate sentence as a primary goal, the Prisoners Union was largely composed of white ex-cons, led by Willie Holder, a classic Okie robber who looked and sounded like a wizened version of the musician Willie Nelson. Also around were John Irwin, a '50s era robber who'd gone on to become a sociology professor at San Francisco State, Frank Smith, a literate one-time drug dealer and kidnapper—surprisingly gentle and good-willed given his biker-qua-mountain-man persona—and Roney Nunes, who'd served time in the midwest for a crime that he'd later proven he had not committed only to pull off a bungled robbery in California for which he'd done a few years. Other than Willie's wife Patty, the Union in the early '70s had almost no women in positions of authority. Deftly using the credibility of Irwin, the persistence of Holder, and the reasoning skills of Smith, the Prisoners Union had gotten the ear of several legislators, some lawyers (notably Jim Smith and Michael Snedecker) and had received the gift of a large but rundown building on San Francisco's Potrero Hill from an elderly sympathizer. Holder and his wife lived upstairs (always with a few recent parolees and occasionally someone like Snedecker whose choices as a lawyer kept him as close to a street person as a practicing advocate could be).

The UPU stood in sharp contrast with its leadership focused entirely on the charismatic nature of Jackson, an African American from rural Louisiana with the thickest accent I'd ever heard. Off the record, the Prisoners Union's rap on Jackson was that he'd been a snitch in the joint and was an empty-headed idiot interested only in sex with white women and ripping off the Stanford students of the Venceremos Brigade who helped to fund his organization. The UPU's position on the Prisoners Union was that it was run by hill-billy white racists, one step removed from the Aryan Brotherhood,[23] who were using their connections to liberal politicians to angle for grants. The UPU argued that all felons were involved in class war whether they understood it as such or not and that band-aid measures like administrative due process in internal disciplinary procedures or the replacement of the indeterminate sentence by a more systematic (and thereby more "fair") structure of penalties for crimes only served to strengthen the system and slow the progress toward a necessary revolution that would be led not by college-trained leftists, but by former prisoners who had had direct experience within "the belly of the beast."

I had friends in both organizations although relatively few seemed to understand what I thought I was doing working in the prison movement. (In 1976, Holder, who by then had known me for five years, asked me "well, just what did you serve time for?") In 1972, when I began working with CPHJ, it had been clear to me for at least two years that no revolution was even remotely in the offing in the United States and I had no illusions that the working class people of Concord or Alamo or anywhere were about to follow somebody who's greatest accomplishment may have been a bungled liquor store robbery.

Still, it was (and is) true that economic crime carries within it a domain of the irrational that was and always will be about class. The women around the UPU were not only neither idiots nor dupes, and were some of the most intelligent people I would ever meet in the prison movement. For the most part they all came from the very lowest fringes of the working class—a position with which I immediately identified—and some would go on to significant careers as lawyers and private eyes.

Popeye was another matter. A shrewd political thinker with a mercurial temper, he played all sides against one another, even within his own organization, which recycled people in purges and counter-purges. One time Marti asked me to help her move from her apartment in the Mission, a move dictated by Popeye after it had decided that there must be FBI infiltrators in the group.[24] Each of the collective houses and apartments that UPU members shared were to be broken up as they were to find housing with people outside the movement altogether. When I arrived at Marti's apartment, there were guns on the kitchen table, set there just so people would feel comfortable enough to cooperate in getting a couch down a flight of stairs.

Marti soon left not only the organization but the Bay Area, settling in the Sierra foothills in hopes that her husband would not find her. Two years later, Popeye Jackson was murdered in the front seat of his car, parked in front of his apartment on Albion Street in San Francisco. Shot alongside him was a young schoolteacher from the Contra Costa suburbs who'd been active with the UPU for only a few weeks.

With a shotgun and "in defense" the officer shot him in the face.

If one has a shotgun, defenses purposes do not require you to aim at the head of the other party. This was the report given in the media concerning the capture of a bank robber, treated as though without question or controversy.

Here, for a moment, we are joined.

It took me, it seems, forever to reach out to your mother. Peggy had moved out of the flat on San Jose Avenue in the Mission District some six months before, after which I'd had a short and profoundly unfulfilling relationship with an Australian painter and performance artist, Jill Scott.

I had worked for a year on an ethnography of the Tenderloin for Central City Hospitality House. The project team needed an administrator, having hired one only to have him quit in a huff and hurry, so were delighted when I literally walked in one day, able to handle that work, edit the final report and interview the one neighborhood group the two primary researchers, Toby Marotta and Clark Taylor, felt nervous about—ex-felons. Marotta and Taylor were interested in the Tenderloin's gay history, but it was the entire community that was to be described by the project. By design, two members of the team were neighborhood residents, one of whom, Dorothy Rutherford, a one-time fashion model and one of the last true hippies, had promptly moved herself and her four-year-old son out to Bernal Heights where she shared a flat with two other women who worked at the agency, Kathy Ryan and Krishna Evans. At the time, Ms. Evans directed the arts program on the agency's main floor, a large open studio crafts and fine arts workshop that funded itself by asking participants to make two of anything they worked on and to donate one item for sale through a "store" that consisted of the agency's Leavenworth Street windows.

She had impossibly thick, long black hair with just the slightest threading of silver, which she wore pulled back in a failed attempt to look plain. She wore oversized army pants and tank top t-shirts, never with a bra. More important, she had (has) the most complete smile I have ever seen.[25] Although our programs only occasionally had direct business with one another, it was evident hat she was a passionate administrator who cared deeply about her students and took her job with absolute seriousness. She was capable of great theater in staff meetings, raging out, slamming the door behind her. Once, the director of the drop-in center upstairs, a man who often came to work smelling of wine, pawed a high school coed who was interning in the arts program. Krishna walked up to him, flattened him with a single punch (several metal folding chairs crashing out of the way as he falls backward). She stormed upstairs to the executive director's office and got the man fired on the spot.

Because Hospitality House defined itself as a place open to anyone, regardless of how marginal, the various floors were always full of street people, runaways, ex-cons, drag queens, psychotics, confused post-docs, alcoholics, junkies, the works. For awhile, our receptionist was Jerry-Diane, a pre-op transsexual whose goal in life was to become a lesbian. It was, and I mean this literally, the finest working environment I have ever had, can ever imagine having.

Early on in my tenure with the ethnographic project, Peg and I had been invited over for brunch to the house on Bernal Heights, along with several other HH staffers. The house on Winfield Street was a rambling Victorian set high into the hillside. I remember the weather that day as perfect and a sense of life there as almost utopian. In retrospect, I'm sure what that meant was that I was attracted to all three of the women who lived there. It was already apparent to both Peggy and me that this latest attempt to construct a relationship was proving a disaster.

Once or twice a week after work, Dorothy, Krishna and I, occasionally with one or two other members of the staff, would head over to Harrington's, a cavernous Irish pub only a block from HH, where we'd sit, drinking watery draft beer or gin and tonics, eating hotdogs and popcorn, talking office politics for hours. Dorothy, who'd lived for several years in Spain and several full grown sons there, often brought along her four-year-old boy, Jose.

Once, at an agency picnic, I sat on the grass and Krishna (without asking, without being asked) lay back to put her head in my lap. My heart raced a million miles. Another time, one of the neighborhood men, Eugeia Shaw, celebrated his 25th birthday at a Castro Street pizza parlor, after which Krishna and I took the longest of walks back through the mission. She pointed out Hungadunga, which had been the leading commune in the free food family and where she'd had several friends and a few lovers.

I had a prohibition in my head about sleeping with my co-workers. I was insecure enough about employment generally to feel that some crossing of the boundaries like that would certainly make life crazy. Although I'd more than a few unrequited crushes on women in other organizations of the prison movement, I'd virtually fled the apartment of Jeanne Baker, a young single mother who volunteered for CPHJ, not because I wasn't attracted, but because I was.

When the ethnographic project came to an end with the publication of "TERP Report," the five of us on the project were duly laid off. I'd already proposed to Claudia Viek, the executive director of Hospitality House, that what the neighborhood needed, more than anything else, was a positive self-image. Some of the folks in the upstairs drop-in center had started a mimeographed publication called the *Tenderloin Times*. They'd published three issues with runs of about 150 each, until somebody on the board discovered a recipe for mistletoe tea and had flipped at the idea of the toxic possibilities. I'd suggested that I could take over the paper, turn it into a real neighborhood paper just like the *Bernal Journal* or *Potrero View*, and sell enough advertising to cover the printing costs. Since that wouldn't provide enough work (or cash) to make a real job out of the position, I suggested that I run a writers workshop, trying to get funding from the California Arts Council for that, and that I also work on housing issues in the neighborhood with funding from the agency itself.

I felt ambivalent about the idea. Krishna had given me several hints that, if she ever broke up with her current boyfriend, an itinerant and seldom-employed rock musician who periodically went by the name Random Chance, she'd be available and was interested. We'd ride buses to the Haight after work, she on her way to class at USF, me on my way to the Grand Piano, and increasingly our conversations turned to relationships and what each of us was seeking. We never actually said out loud that it was each other we were talking about.

It was apparent that this woman was brilliant, beautiful, had a sense of the arts (she'd studied ballet with Balanchine and Cunningham), was committed to her work and the people of the neighborhood she served. A cousin of hers, Julie Garrett, was visiting San Francisco and would come to the Writers Workshop, hanging around afterwards to ride on the Mission Street bus with me. Julie would tell me, at length, that Krishna was interested in me, but was afraid that I might be too intellectual. At other times, Dorothy and Steve Brady also dropped similar hints.

Peggy had long since returned from Georgia and the abortion, moving to an apartment directly across the street from the one we'd shared on San Jose Avenue. "If I'm the one who moves," she said, "I won't feel like I was the one who was dumped." I moped around for a few weeks, then, at a music performance at Mills, I ran into an Australian artist by the name of Jill Scott, whom I knew very slightly through Carla Harryman. Jill and I talked and later I ran into her again after a performance in the City. We got involved soon after, although it devolved almost instantly. I was looking for a relationship and she absolutely seemed terrified by the idea. I was restless.

A month after the job at the Ethnographic Project ended, one of the administrators at HH quit, leaving a small, part-time salary. Claudia called and asked me to start work on the new position, waiting until we heard from the Arts Council to pick up the other segments. The truth was, I hadn't even begun to look for another job yet. Instead, I'd spent the month watching the relationship with Jill devolve, had done a performance I'd been thinking about for a year at least, reading all of *Ketjak* aloud on the steps of the Bank of America branch at Powell and Market Streets, three days after which I had had a tooth extracted. The oral surgeon had told me I would need a ride home afterwards, so I'd asked Dorothy, one of the few people I knew who owned a car (a clunker that cost maybe $200). As I'd woken groggy from the anesthesia, Krishna stood over me, explaining ex post facto that she thought it would be "fun to help."

I accepted the position.

One evening six weeks later, on my way to Bruce Boone's for a meeting of the Marxist study group that we were in together, a young woman next to me on the Mission Street bus asked about the book I was reading, Georg Lukács' *History and Class Consciousness*. I'd been writing notes in the margins and underlining passages in several different colors of ink.[26] She nodded as I explained what I was doing, asked who Lukács was, and, after she "debused," suddenly ran back up to my window shouting her phone number. I called the next day and we went to lunch at Knight's on Golden Gate Avenue, a giant old-style cafeteria that catered to the City Hall and lawyer set. Laura was working as a legal secretary for Charles Garry, a criminal defense specialist I knew slightly from my work at CPHJ, but thought of herself as a folk singer between gigs. "Before gigs," she corrected herself, laughing.

As we ate and I slowly began to realize that the excitement of a chance encounter on the bus hadn't led to any sort of miracle, in walked Dan White with a couple of his aides. White had just resigned from his position as a San Francisco County Supervisor, unable to make ends meet on his $9,000 a year salary—I could hardly blame him—but had just changed his mind and was trying in vain to convince Mayor Moscone to re-appoint him to his same old seat. White had been in the headlines for weeks and I was surprised that Laura didn't seem to know who he was.

It was only a day or so later that, as I attended a political conference at Horace Mann School in the Mission, I first heard of the massacre at Jonestown. Garry was down in Guyana representing Jim Jones, the charismatic San Francisco preacher who'd become increasingly paranoid and hostile, leading his congregation literally into the jungle. He'd arranged for a visit by Leo Ryan, a Congressman from San Mateo County and a former paper member of the CPHJ board. Among Ryan's entourage was a photographer from the *San Francisco Examiner*, Greg Robinson, who'd recently finished doing a feature on Krishna's program at HH. Both were killed in the attack on the visitors at the airstrip as they'd attempted to depart. As Jones and his followers began to drink poisoned Kool-Aid, Garry slipped into the woods to hide. In a matter of an hour, over 900 people were dead.

I felt sick the minute I heard the first details. Like anyone on the left in San Francisco, I'd run into People's Temple members dozens, perhaps hundreds of times, usually help-ing out with the Saturday precinct work alongside the New American Movement, DSOC and the unions. Ryan, a former schoolteacher who'd once spent a week "undercover" in prison just to get a feel for the environment (and not part as a media grandstanding stunt), was that rare individual, someone motivated into politics by the idea of accomplishing something.

The next week was Thanksgiving. I found myself in that tortured state of needing to read every word in the media about Jonestown, feeling increasingly nauseated the more I read. On Monday or Tuesday, Dorothy, who was again temping at HH, came down to my office to say that she, Krishna and Kathy were going to have a meal of Thanksgiving leftovers on Friday and did I want to join them? She may have invited me to Thanksgiving itself, but I was already committed to my mother's. A day later, Dorothy again dropped by to say that she and Kathy were planning to go to the movies later that night "so that it will just be you and Krishna, if that's okay." More than a little amused by the transparency of this set-up, I accepted.

The next two days gave me time to think. I'd had what seemed excellent reasons not to get involved with Krishna. There was the work taboo. She was, she said, still involved to some degree with this musician, although she'd also hinted on several occasions that she was looking to move on. As it stood, our relationship wasn't predicated on my life as a poet. Peg had been the first woman in my life for whom that had not been, if not the paramount fact about me, at least an important one. And Peg had been jealous of my writing in a way that had surprised me. If Barbara had been merely envious of the relative success I'd had publishing, a competitive envy, Peggy saw my writing as a relationship in itself, one that would prevent her from ever establishing the sort of balance between us she imagined herself to be seeking. It was impossible to know in advance how Krishna would feel about that. There was no question that I found Krishna desirable and fabulous, but there was also a side of me so anxious I could (rather like a cat) spit. I'd seen her at work under the hectic and often harsh conditions of that environment, dealing with crazies, street people, seniors, city bureaucrats, inept board members, the corporate types on the United Way review committee. On one occasion a client tried to kill her, attempting to ram her with a ladder—she remained magically calm under the threat, turned by the event into pure concentration itself, never once allowing her assaulter to imagine himself in control, talking him into a form of submission while I and John Denning, an art teacher, physically stopped the ladder each time this speed-crazed young man roared forward.[27] I'd also seen a harder side at work also, the flashing temper and take-no-prisoners insistence on honesty. Unlike my situation with Jill, where I'd hopped into bed with no hesitation, knowing that there would be few lasting consequences if it didn't work out,[28] I could sense that Krishna would be exactly the opposite. If I got involved, it would have to be all the way.

On Friday at dusk, I walked the mile from the apartment I now shared with Fred Glass over to Krishna's. An index of my anxiety and sense of anticipation that evening is that I can still recall the precise quality of twilight along Mission as I walked, stopping once or twice to write down sentences in a notebook that would later find their way into *Tjanting*. It was a beautiful clear evening, oddly balmy for San Francisco in November. The steep climb up Virginia Street to Winfield, and the ever steeper climb up Winfield, seemed to stretch out forever (I'd only made the trip once or twice before, so wasn't yet familiar with every step).

Dorothy and Kathy wolfed down their dinners, a moist and well-stuffed turkey, and started to head out the door to a movie. But there was a catch—cousin Julie, who had become a semi-permanent house guest, staying in a room nominally devoted to weaving equipment, decided (I forget why) not to go along, even though Dorothy and Kathy offered to pay her way. Given the layout of the house, two tiny bedrooms by the front door, beyond which was a huge, central kitchen, with a dark, windowless alcove that nominally served as the living room, stairs up to an attic-like loft that was Dorothy's space, and on the other side the room that had become Julie's space all focused around a large, round kitchen table, there was virtually no way to be in the house without being in Julie's presence, unless Krishna and I were to retire to her bedroom (too loaded with anticipation, lust and symbolism) or Julie were to retire to hers (too clueless to figure this out).[29] So we sat around the table and talked for several hours. I have no memory whatsoever what about.

At midnight, I noted the time and Krishna suggested that the two of us walk around the top of Bernal Hill, a rare blister of open space in San Francisco, topped with a huge microwave dish for the phone company. Although three of the most economically depressed housing projects are within a short walk of this mile-long unlit, half-paved circular road, we thought nothing of heading off into the darkness on that warm night and found only two or three cars with teenage couples parked overlooking the Mission. We walked slowly and talked, although even at this point we did not touch. I could sense from Krishna's body language that she wanted me to reach over to her, but that she wouldn't or couldn't do that herself. My mind was racing a million miles an hour as I remembered every reason why I did or didn't want to act. Eventually we got back to her front stairs, where we paused silently for what seemed like minutes.

"Would you like to come in for tea?"

"Why not?" Trying to sound casual. In fact, it is only now that I realize I've decided, not so much that I've made a decision but rather that I recognize a decision I've arrived at on some level almost inaccessible to me.

Inside again, I'm immediately relieved to discover that Julie has finally gone to bed. Kathy and Dorothy are still out, but for how long? For the moment at least, we're alone in the kitchen. Krishna moves to brush past me to put a kettle on for tea and I reach out my arms, palms up. She takes my hands and without the slightest hesitation sits in my lap, which surprises me but feels wonderful. We kiss.

"So what are your intentions?"

"Why don't we discuss this in your bedroom?"

Eventually, that is exactly what we do, another long conversation, only now at least it is Krishna who is being infinitely cautious, hesitant about going forward. Her reaction to my reaching out is more one of relief than desire. I'm trying very hard to understand and read these subtle signs. Already we've crossed over emotional boundaries we won't ever be able to re-erect. I want to make love, but she's not ready, she says. "Lets just sleep." So we do, me entirely naked, her still in tank top and blue jeans.

At dawn or just before, I wake and lean over and kiss her gently. She's awake also, although maybe I don't realize this at first. Without a word, she slowly rises and stands over me on the narrow bed, removing her clothes. This is the closest thing to a vision I will ever have.

We make love twice, taking almost until noon to finish. When we finally stumble toward the kitchen, Kathy and Dorothy are at the table, laughing that they'd gotten up in the morning, realized I must still be there and had headed out of the house to give us privacy. They've returned hours later post-brunch and we're still in bed and they'd begun to wonder if we would ever rise. We eat a cursory breakfast and say very little. We're exhausted and shy and exhilarated. I feel as though I've used a lifetime of adrenaline—it would be easy to hallucinate. After the meal settles us down somewhat, we walk very casually back to my apartment on San Jose where we spend the afternoon in bed.

It is only because I've promised to attend a book party at Geoff Young's in Berkeley that I ever really rise at all that day, at dusk, because Tom Mandel's coming by to give me a ride. Krishna and I dress and we sit on my minuscule back porch overlooking the minuscule Poplar Alley until the bell rings. As Krishna says good bye and heads up the hill, Tom looks at my poor dazed expression and says, "What hit you?"

It would make sense, narratively, to stop right here, but life is not a plot. On Monday morning, I wake and rise at Krishna's. We decide (or maybe it's Krishna who decided this) that she should go into work first and that we shouldn't arrive together. Later, as I'm riding the Mission bus down past DuBoce, somebody who's been playing a boom box turns the volume full blast. I hear the words "Mayor Moscone and Supervisor Harvey Milk have been shot and are presumed dead this morning at City Hall," and then the sound is turned back down again. No further explanation. The words sound completely foreign and meaningless at first. I've known George Moscone since I first worked for CPHJ and he sat on the Senate Judiciary Committee. I've known Harvey Milk because everyone in San Francisco knew Harvey Milk. In a moment the bus turns onto Van Ness and when it reaches City Hall, I get off. I walk inside past no security whatsoever and see Bill Kraus, Harvey's aide and a DSOC activist, red-eyed, talking to a crowd. Rudy Nothenberg, one of Moscone's assistants, is running full tilt up the broad stairs. Police are everywhere. TV cameras are everywhere. Why am I here?

I walk outside again, down Golden Gate Avenue two blocks and the one block up Leavenworth to Hospitality House. As always, the step from the brilliant sunlight of the street (made all the more stark by these treeless Tenderloin stucco facades) into the shadows of the arts center is almost blinding. I wait for my eyes to adjust to the dark. Nobody's working—everyone is just standing around, talking. They've already heard. I remembered seeing flowers already sprinkled on the steps of City Hall as I'd left and I suggest that we should buy some also and take them there. Several of us head out to purchase roses from a street vendor near Harrington's. By now City Hall is secured and closed, so we stand around the broad stairs, Krishna and I and Dorothy and Spider and I don't remember who else. It's a beautiful sunny afternoon. It's a terrible day. The headlines in the newspaper boxes are still filled with Jonestown.

Krishna had already planned to leave the following weekend for Baltimore and Virginia where a sister is getting married. It feels as if we spend the week itself attending one memorial service after another. It's an insane time and I feel wildly out of sync to be so intensely aroused and pleased every single minute of it. The morning she flies off we stand at the top of the Esmerelda Steps, one of the great secret views of the city, not long after sunrise, talking about how we'll write to one another.[30] We already know (have known for months) that talk, casual, intimate, intelligent conversation, will be an important form for us. It will be a long time before many other important things occur. Over four years, for example, before either one of us really settles into monogamy. Another six before I stop drinking. Eight before we marry. Eleven before Krishna nearly dies from an ectopic pregnancy. Twelve before I begin to go blind from cataracts. Thirteen before you are born. Sixteen before we all move to Pennsylvania. But in more ways than an individual could hope to understand, the logic that leads through each of those events was already implicit (though not inherent) the instant I said yes to a cup of tea. I crossed a line in my life from which I have never stepped back.

This, in a sense, is the exact opposite of telos, but rather a recognition that choice is central to freedom. With both its intended and unintended consequences.

I remember a day fourteen years earlier when, 17 years old, my highschool flat-top just starting to grow out, I was walking through Newport, RI, wondering what to do in the next 48 hours when the annual folk festival would begin and my room at the local "Y" would go instead to someone with a reservation. I looked to the left as I crossed the intersection, noticed a small coffeehouse and thought to walk in. Asking to speak to the manager, I inquired if they needed any assistance for the festival week and that I'd happily accept meals and a place to sleep. Can you perform, I was asked. I lied, saying that I could do stand-up comedy. I only had to do one set during the week, possibly because I was dreadful at it.[31] But this was enough not only to give me shelter, literally a palette on the floor, but also access to some backstage parties connected to the festival. Which was how I found myself sitting next to Bob Dylan on a couch one night as he and Paul Stookey and Sebastian Dangerfield improvized a version of "King Bee." I'd never heard of the British rock group whose record Buffy Sainte-Marie told me this song had been found on, but sensed that I was being given the most privileged of "inside" information. What if, I thought to myself, I hadn't looked to the left when I'd crossed that street?

That night in 1978, with Krishna already thousands of miles away, I'm walking alone through a human sea of candles in the shabby urban park in front of City Hall, hyper-conscious in this first separation that the same dynamics are now being played out in my life on a whole other scale. I'm overwhelmed by all of the visible grief I see around me in this memorial rally held both for the assassinations and the mass suicide in Guyana. And I'm overwhelmed by the vertigo of love. I understand already that I'm involved far more than I've ever been before, that I've arrived at a whole new level of risk. So the same thought recurs: *What if?* And, *How much courage will I have to see this through?* On a stage mounted over the City Hall steps, Joan Baez is singing *Amazing Grace.*

The want-ads lie strewn on the table.

It is not possible to "describe a life."

Notes

* From *ABC* (Berkeley: Tuumba 46, 1983). "Albany" first appeared in *Ironwood* 20 (Tucson: Fall 1982) vol. 10, no. 2, pp. 112–113.

1 While Arnold told me, when I ran into him at a reading of Kit Robinson's and Rae Armantrout's at San Francisco State in 1992, that "I was *so* in love with Susan Hughes," his text described her as picking at the hair on her arms, a comment that must have radiated with the gender and racial anxieties of the 1950s in a working-class suburb that actively sought to keep ethnic minorities out.

2 I never thanked Vance Teague for the gift of this lesson (although I have Arnold), other than by way of a brief note on the web site for Albany High alumni. According to Al Nielsen, my 6th grade teacher, Teague retired after suffering a heart attack several years later.

3 The Marin-Sonoma suburban system that came into being the week I started my job at CPHJ in February, 1972, replacing a previous Greyhound system.

4 Although I write significant portions of *Ketjak* in transit, the first poem I will complete entirely on the bus is *Sitting Up, Standing, Taking Steps*. *The Chinese Notebook* was also written entirely on Golden Gate Transit. By 1976, just two years after I first begin writing daily on transit, I write *BART*, a work premised entirely on the transit system upon which it was penned. After I leave CPHJ in the fall of '76, my writing again becomes more varied in terms of the circumstances of its composition, although I continue to use transit regularly through 1986 (when I finally learn to drive).

5 The name the US Post Office gives to San Quentin.

6 In retrospect, I realize just how few of even these poets would
   have agreed with me then.

7 In the last years I lived in Berkeley, Krishna and I would meet
   people at Cafe Roma in that same location. Our behavior with
   our friends over upscale pastries differed from my great uncle's
   principally in style.

8 Several of the sections that were merely guessed at or barely
   sketched out when the chart was drafted have now been
   completed or are nearing completion, and "Y" has become *You*.

9 As it turned out, although I didn't realize this for almost a year,
   Richie was also the kid brother of playwright and novelist Len
   Jenkin.

10 Eventually it would be her desire for children that would move
   our relationship away from the sexual. She wanted to be certain
   that her husband was the father. Twenty years later, this woman
   is still one of my two or three closest friends.

11 It has no vistas and you cannot see the ocean even from the peak
   of its lone hill.

12 In the late '40s, when it was already apparent just how debased
   the Communist Party had become, Ev and Val been infatuated
   with Mao, some of whose ideas still wafted through the air of
   the office, the entire idea of a project of recreating consciousness, "socialist man." By 1971, when I first met her, they'd
   decided to focus specifically on local issues and had spent most
   of the previous decade running the United Farm Worker
   support organization in Marin County. They'd met sometime
   around, perhaps during, the Oakland general strike in the 1940s.
   She'd spent the war "double-bottoming" boats with asbestos
   insulation, protecting them in theory from torpedoes.

13 To whom *Garfield* is dedicated.

14 House Un-American Activities Committee.

15 With the exception of a couple of dates early in my career in the
   prison movement, I never got involved with women I met
   through my political work, in part because in there were so few.
   But also because even as I worked long hours every day that

world for years, I was always, first and foremost, a poet. It was to my life and needs as a writer to which any woman would eventually have to adjust.

16 By now at least, having been "freed" of my alternative service obligation by virtue of the fact that I, and every other conscientious objector of that same period, had been "drafted" and inducted unlawfully, at a time when others were not being called, CPHJ now took it upon itself to pay this directly, where the previous year I'd worked nights doing layout and paste-up and miscellaneous writing for a small gay bar paper in San Francisco.

17 The Moscone Center, hotels and museums dominate the neighborhood today.

18 The community services that were supposed to supplant them were never funded. Who ever imagined that they would be?

19 I was expelled from the squad after I'd locked a seventh grade bully into a school locker.

20 An example: every Tuesday afternoon I update a series of charts that track the stock performance of several companies that perform desktop services.

21 As has been increasingly evident, the state itself is merely a convenience. Capital and its latest expression, "information," are more powerful and fundamentally stateless phenomena. The creation of the European Union is itself a desperate attempt for several governments, formerly "world powers," to reimagine themselves as relevant.

22 The same strategy domestically was carried out under the banner of Cointelpro.

23 One or two of the ex-cons who cycled briefly through the Prisoners Union went on to people local Klan groups.

24 This was absolutely the case. Sara Jane Moore was revealed as an informant after her attempted assassination of Gerald Ford. The FBI wanted to know why my phone number at CPHJ was in her address book.

25 This same smile, Colin, appears miraculously on your own shin-
    ing face.

26 Looking at the book today, I see, on the inside front cover, in a
    black box, "Opacity 159." In orange, above, "Art begets dialects
    begets history 137–145." In red, below, "The production of new
    needs = the accumulation of SURPLUS VALUE 180!" In blue, to
    the right, "Aura as a bourgeois (unmediated) element in art 158!"

27 What had set Eric, an unemployed African American with a
    family crammed into a small hotel room on Mason Street, off
    was another HH client who'd called him *nigger*. The staff in the
    upstairs drop-in center had rescued that idiot, but had done so
    by diverting Eric, who was literally exploding with anger and
    meth-amphetamine, down to the arts floor where he'd gone
    after the first white person he saw, Krishna. As 50 or so people
    surrounded us, it was evident that Eric was, in the eyes of many,
    the victim in this scenario, so that Krishna, John and I all under-
    stood that we needed to resolve the circumstance not only with-
    out anyone getting hurt, but without Eric getting arrested
    either. Around the corner, out of sight, the SF police waited it
    out, which took a good two hours. They thought we were crazy.
    But it ended with Eric going out with John and me for a cup of
    coffee to talk about why anger and speed mixed badly.

28 It would be another three-plus years before city housing special-
    ist Dick Gamble, the first AIDS victim in my circle, began to
    grow thin and pale.

29 Worse yet, there was a downstairs apartment, a small separate
    unit, in which the erstwhile-musician/boyfriend lived!

30 I will send her a letter that takes up the whole of a Chinese note-
    book, a favorite form of mine in the mid-'70s, which she still has
    somewhere. She writes me a long detailed description of the
    wedding.

31 I plagiarized my material from the dim memory of an old Alan
    Sherman record.

Printed in the United States
28360LVS00001B/440